MOVIN'ON

USING MOMENTS OF CHALLENGE AS A SPRINGBOARD TO BECOMING MORE

ROD RAYMOND

(M.Ed.)

Author of *Quick Fit* and *Raisin Cake: Lessons Learned from Grandma*

D0907523

Rod Raymond's long-awaited book *Movin' On* creatively shares with you easy to follow strategies for overcoming the challenges in your life. Rod leads you away from the negative energy and problems you may have run up against towards more mindful reflection.

While studying for his doctorate with some of the best and brightest gurus in transpersonal psychology, Rod learned how effective a purposeful and energetic mindfulness practice can be in transforming lives. In this book, Rod challenges you with stories, powerful mindfulness techniques, and strategies you can implement to immediately become a better version of yourself.

If you are going through some challenging life situations, your opportunity for lasting change is now! This book will take you high, and it will take you low. You will learn to retrain your inner voice and control the mystical energy that creates success and happiness. After all, it is your life — live it subconsciously on purpose!

Also by Rod Raymond

Raisin Cake: Lessons Learned from Grandma
Quick Fit
Advanced Marathon Training
Advanced 1/2 Marathon Training
Beginner Marathon Training
Beginner 1/2 Marathon Training

MOVIN' ON

USING MOMENTS OF
CHALLENGE
AS A SPRINGBOARD
TO BECOMING MORE

ROD RAYMOND
(M.Ed.)

Author of *Quick Fit* and *Raisin Cake: Lessons Learned from Grandma*

To my boys — Beau and Jack

ISBN: 978-0-9718820-1-0

Design: Bill Ramsey

ACKNOWLEDGMENTS

I want to thank all my teachers, mentors and friends who helped me with this book. Robert Lillegard, Teri Glembin, Erin Dewitt, Rosslyn Kendrick, Jess Koski and others. Navigating this process has been both a cathartic and powerful experience. Thank you all so much!

FOREWORD

I have known Rod Raymond for a few years now. We met while taking psychology classes together at the Institute of Transpersonal Psychology. I noticed him in class before we were formerly introduced. His radiant energy struck me as someone whose path I was meant to cross. As I have gotten to know him, my instincts have been confirmed. Rod possesses a level of awareness that is fascinating to watch. I have learned that the depth of his authenticity and the genuineness of his optimism are not the product of an easy life, but rather his conscious decision to turn pain into opportunity. He states in *Movin' On*, "Change your story. Change your pain. Differentiate the pain that hurts you from the pain that changes you." Rod shares countless personal stories in *Movin' On* to inspire the reader to believe by his example that our power lies in our right to choose how we experience and tell our story. Beliefs are agreements we make with reality. The MOA's suggested in this book will assist the reader in exploring what some of their underlying beliefs are, why we made those agreements, and how we can strengthen the agreements that support us as well as change the agreements that no longer serve us or the collective.

If you are or ever have gone through an experience in which you felt life was over or there was no promise for a positive outcome, this book is a must read."

I have been teaching psychology for 15 years and never have I met a human being so hungry to learn and so willing to share. *Movin' On* is filled from cover to cover with priceless advice. Not only does Rod present to the reader a succinct synthesis of psychological and self-help philosophies, but he also explains to each reader how to actualize this information easily into one's daily routine through a variety of meditative practices. Not only does he teach us why, but he also shows us how to cultivate awareness. Rod Raymond's *Movin' On* is alchemy for the conscious creator.

> ❝
> **The secret is to move beyond the pain of the challenge to the promise of an opportunity. The real tragedy isn't the conflict, it's when you don't let the conflict make your spirit stronger.**❞
>
> —*Rod Raymond*

"The secret is to move beyond the pain of the challenge to the promise of an opportunity," he writes. "The real tragedy isn't the conflict, it's when you don't let the conflict make your spirit stronger."

If you are or ever have gone through an experience in which you felt life was over or there was no promise for a positive outcome, this book is a must read. Rod shows us how to transform our challenges into strengths that will springboard us into opportunities, which will lead us in directions that sometimes surpass, in the most positive ways, our wildest expectations.

In addition, Rod teaches us a number of different meditation tools we can practice in order to strengthen and expand our breadth of conscious awareness. He then shares that there are only two types of moments: moments we love and moments we learn from. As we ebb and flow through these moments without resistance, we find our purpose and path unfolding before us, inviting us toward authenticity, joy and enlightenment. As we progress through our ascent, it's also important to understand our evolving wisdom looks less like climbing a ladder and more like widening the beam of a flashlight. *Movin' On* is a tool that helps us do just that.

Tharwat Fahoum Lovett, MAP
Emotional Wellness Coach

HOW TO USE THIS BOOK

READ THE "5 TYPES OF MEDITATION"

Like most books of this nature, *Movin' On* is only as good as one's ability to do something with the knowledge gained. Contemplative practices take many forms. There are literally thousands of ways to integrate a mindfulness practice, and in the notes section at the end of this book I share five ways that I believe to be the most effective.

MOVIN' ON ACTIONS (MOA)

As you are reading along, you will come across *Movin' On* Actions (MOAs). These "right now" actions are designed to shift your thinking away from being a casual reader to becoming an active one making conscious changes. Don't blow these off. You may find them to be the most valuable takeaways in this book.

SHARE WHAT YOU LEARN

There's an old saying: "The one who teaches, learns the most." If a thought or idea resonated with you, and a friend or family member's face popped up while you were reading or meditating on that thought, they may need to hear from you. It wasn't a coincidence their image came to you.

HAVE FUN!

I wrote this with one goal in mind: to help you move toward a space that nurtures joy. This practical, quick read is designed to give you tools to help you on the path to optimal wellness. Open your mind, heart, and body to allow these ideas to guide you on your journey to discover the authentic "you."

EXPERIENCE

There is no coming to consciousness without pain.
—C.G. Jung

As a professional speaker, business owner, and international endurance athlete, I've encountered many people and experienced much success in life. I've also experienced my share of dark people and gloomy moments. After enduring hardship several years ago, I sat down to talk with a good friend, and she shared something very wise with me. She likened me to a butterfly that had been placed back in its cocoon. She explained that for a butterfly to become strong enough to handle the challenges of the world, it needed to struggle and to fight to get out of its cocoon. If someone were to cut the cocoon and let the butterfly out too early, it would not have enough strength and would surely die. I needed to get stronger, wiser, embrace my experience, and push through my crucible. Eventually, I broke out of my cocoon, and, while life still brings challenges, I am free. Maya Angelou, the American poet, memoirist, and civil rights activist, once remarked: "We delight in the beauty of the butterfly, but rarely admit the changes it has gone through to achieve that beauty."

I am movin' on!

EVERYTHING MATTERS.

We all have experiences as participants in this thing called life. Whether these experiences are big or small, positive or negative, they influence who you are, and, moreover, who you will be. Let me start by saying: every experience, big or small, matters. The fool says, "Told the boss a little white lie, so I could go fishing with my buddies, no big deal." Well, even if the boss doesn't find out, we have begun the process of rewiring our mind. Before we know it, we're telling bigger lies and defending ourselves more and more. Key phrase: EVERYTHING MATTERS!

If we are human, then we have had an experience that hurt us a great deal—a divorce/breakup, death of a loved one, being bullied, getting fired, or a health ailment. As a result, we may have experienced a certain level of depression. When we are happy, we "vibrate" at a very high level. When depressed, that vibration begins to wane. Before we know it, we are low energy people that no one wants to be around. We may say, "Why aren't my co-workers, family and friends recognizing that I am hurting here? Why aren't they calling me up to ask me how I am doing?" Again, everything matters! How we respond to life frames our happiness. There is no other way to look at it. Increasing our awareness can save our lives.

CONSIDER THIS ...

Try to recall a life event that totally shook you up and got you feeling depressed. Naturally, your personal vibration for your life-force energy declined; you felt "low." In your depressed state, you went to work. Eventually the boss got frustrated with you because your low energy was not productive. At home, your low vibration didn't afford you the space to deal with normal family issues, and you acted out of character toward those you love. Before you knew it, family members were avoiding you or not engaging with you at all. This situation got you feeling sorry for yourself. You didn't call up your friends, and, because you had become a "drainer," they didn't call you either. You felt totally alone. Perhaps you started eating junk food and drinking more to escape the pain. You became fat and out of shape, further feeding your depression, and so on. Can you identify with this scenario or any part of it?

HANG OUT WITH A FAMILY MEMBER OR FRIEND WHO IS VIBRATING AT A HIGHER LEVEL.

As you may recall from your elementary-school music class, striking a key of C tuning fork on the table will cause all key of C tuning forks around it to vibrate. However, it won't make the key of A-minor vibrate, or any other key. If the key of C represents happy energy and the key of

---
MOVIN' ON ACTION

Just in case you quit reading after this page, I want to give you a very powerful solution right now. Pick up the phone and purposefully connect with a family member or friend who is vibrating at a higher level than you, and just hang out. Be open to their positivity and simply be with them. Write down the names of two such people you could call right now:

_____

_____

A-minor represents low, depressed energy, you need to be around "Cs" more. The good news is you are not a hardened steel tuning fork that cannot change vibrations. You are a malleable, dynamic, sentient being, and you can change. Take the Beach Boys' advice and find those "good vibrations." Absorb and become the key of C! This metaphor has many applications, as you will discover in the pages to come.

We all can reflect on our lives and the amazing opportunities and challenges that have inspired our spirits . However, as we all know, life doesn't always go as planned. We all have ups and downs.

Some ups are really up, and some downs are really down. Unlike Chris Farley in his famed "Saturday Night Live" skit, "The Motivational Speaker," most have never lived in "a van down by the river." However, we all have had a challenge or an event that made us feel like we would rather be in that van, alone and away from others, to avoid the pain. I know I have felt that way. The good news is we can all embrace those moments when we feel like the cocoon is squeezing in on us and use it to get stronger and wiser. It is time to get movin' on!

WHAT HAPPENS TO YOU HAPPENS TO EVERYONE.

What happens to me, happens to you. What happens to the animals affects the trees. What happens to the ocean affects your neighbor. What happens at work affects the jungles of the Amazon. We know that the flight of a butterfly in Canada affects the wind patterns in South America. Everything is interconnected.

It is refreshing to think we are not alone; we are not truly bigger than the ant or smaller than the whale. We are in them, and they are in us. We have a shared consciousness.

Whether you have a belief in God or not, maybe you already know that everything is connected, and that what happens to you is really happening for the universe. And if we are in everything, then everything is happening for reasons beyond our wackiest thoughts and wildest imagination.

The universe has a wisdom that transcends our conscious minds. Know this: choosing growth is good for us and leads to the highest kinds of knowledge. The Bible says that all things work together for good and that God will never tempt you beyond what you are able. Even if you do not believe in God, indeed, it does seem that we are not given more than we can handle.

Switching the mind from believing "Bad things always happen to me" to "Things always happen for me" is the first key to movin' on. Believing that personal victory in our lives is in our nature, ensures our ultimate enlightenment.

What I learned from my doctoral studies in psychology and from personal experience is that when one casts negative energy onto others, it usually reflects one's own fundamental darkness or issue. Think of it as reflective psychology. If we get really upset with a colleague at work for something small, perhaps it merely reflects that which is ailing us—be it a negative experience or our own jealousy or envy. If you get mad at your office colleague for being late occasionally, maybe it is because you also tend to be late?

TODAY IS THE DAY TO USE THOSE MOMENTS OF MASSIVE CHALLENGE AS A SPRINGBOARD TO EXPANDING CONSCIOUS AWARENESS.

Becoming aware that we are just sentient beings on this planet—beings who have had experiences designed to catapult us into new sets of values, beliefs, and actions—can be a beautiful thing. If we can find the courage, energy, and awareness to alter our beliefs, we will change our lives. However, we need to be careful of what we become aware of. If we choose the "revenge" mode of awareness, our hair will be gone, we will feed cancer-producing cells, and our friends will abandon us. I don't know about you, but this is not a place I ever want to be!

Purposing joy is a beautiful process. Movin' on is like taking a shower, exercising, and eating—we never "arrive." We need to keep living our practice to build happiness and benefit. Ultimately, everyone would like to be happy, more than anything else in life. Happiness is expanded upon day by day, thought by thought, a tapestry woven moment by moment, worn with joy and transported with us into our next chapter.

IT'S ALL ABOUT THE PROCESS.

As we move toward harmony, we also approach an authentic feeling of wholeness. If we feel a lack of harmony or balance in our lives, understand that it is not permanent and that we can reset our minds.

Perhaps our current life circumstances do not allow for easy change. Once we start retraining the mind, the joy and newfound energy of actualizing our purpose makes getting there less difficult than one might think. Like running a race or taking an important test, being aware that it is not the finish line or the test result that will bring us the joy, but the process of training our bodies or educating our minds, is the most fun.

Having a surprise negative life experience is a big, freaking curveball. Turning what the world sees as pain into an "Aha!" moment is hard, but it is truly beautiful and feels good. We don't need to meditate on a mountaintop or wrap barbed wire around our legs like an Opus Dei member to overcome or recognize our pain. We can rebuild all that is around us simply by changing our beliefs—our mindset. We can heal and re-energize our bodies, rebuild old relationships, and establish new ones. We can find ourselves enjoying our career and hobbies. By simply reframing our minds, we send a clear message to the world around us that we're flowing from one way of living to another. You can reinvent a new, relevant, happy you who projects good energy.

Navigating through this upside down, topsy-turvy world is an opportunity—if we choose to make it one. The real opportunity lies in learning that lifelong skill of rewiring our brains. Once we begin to learn this skill, we can retrain the heart and the mind to respond instead of simply reacting to life's never-ending experiences.

For me, fully embracing life and setting joy as my purpose, is what it's all about now. You or a loved one can be movin' on from your own cocoon if you just get a little bit stronger.

WHO ARE YOU?

Facing fears and having the inner knowledge that we can survive them is a catalyst for living a life filled with amazing joy.

The things we own or use in our lives do not shape us; our experiences shape us. I got a bike for Christmas when I was six years old. It was just a bike. However, when I used the bike, I had many experiences. That thing was a vessel that brought me the freedom to explore many places and connected me with many new friends. Those experiences shaped my feelings and beliefs—beliefs I still carry today—all from a bike! The good news is, we can choose our experiences.

We have all experienced difficult things when we were younger, and sometimes those things come up again later in life. Being aware of which experiences from our past served us well or poorly is a well-kept secret in our brain. Being aware of those secrets—and being able to recognize when our childhood mind, rather than our adult mind, is managing how we respond to what's happening in the present—will allow us to rewire our minds and bring about lasting change.

What happened to us as kids conditioned our childlike minds, and those same childlike thoughts and beliefs continue to be brought to the surface by the things we currently experience. Maybe as a kid, our parents and the kids we hung around with didn't exercise, maybe our parents constantly snapped and yelled at us, or maybe they drank too much. Whatever happened, positively or negatively, it conditioned our young brains to be what they are now.

Let's get practical. How can I know if my possible overreaction to

As we become consciously aware of our thoughts, we can learn to shift them in the direction of our intention. It is at this point that we enter the space of creation."

—*Chantelle Renee*

my spouse's drinking a beer or two is really a reaction to an alcoholic parent, with all the emotions attached to that? How can you know that the happiness you feel when a certain song comes on the radio is because that was the song playing at the high school dance during your first kiss? Regardless, if we know how something relates to our past, if our mind reacts to something that we feel or that others tell us is out of the ordinary, it is possible that this same "something" was attached to an emotional event in our past.

BEING MINDFUL DOES NOT EQUATE TO HAPPINESS.

This may sound strange, but the paradox is that awareness is not necessarily a ticket to greater peace of mind or unlimited happiness. It may even make us sadder or more upset than we were when we weren't aware. But personally, I would rather be awake and have authentic feelings towards life, even if it involves pain, than remain asleep—just a zombie mulling through the day. Ignorance is NOT bliss! Living a dull or "safe" life surely prevents us from "entering the space of creation."

Being aware of our felt response to a situation will help us to know if we need to deal with it. If, in our new state of awareness, we find that reading about global warming or seeing our neighbor dump car oil in the backyard leading down to the stream bothers us more than it did before, we may be driven to act. Mindfulness masters have an uncanny ability to feel the Earth's pain, the pain of animals, and the pain of others. Doing nothing is not an option. Sending compassion and practicing empathy becomes their daily meditation, their intention — their purpose.

Being people of high awareness doesn't mean our past defines us. We shouldn't fret about our past. The good news is, we can learn from the

— **MOVIN' ON ACTION** —

Meditate and write down a "shameful" experience from your past which you believe affects you in the present. How does this experience change the way you see yourself? If necessary, write down how you can forgive yourself for your part in the experience you felt ashamed?

_____

_____

_____

_____

_____

_____

_____

_____

_____

_____

_____

_____

_____

_____

_____

_____

past without living in it. We can recondition our brains right now by practicing non-judgment and focusing on the present. The way we think, act, and feel may have started when we were younger, but now it's time to move past it.

I was listening to NPR the other day when the guest was talking about all the mistakes he had made in his past. He admitted that his mistakes had hurt people and that those mistakes have become very public due to his political life, He went on to say that the most important thing anyone can do to move on from shame and shunning is to go to great lengths to forgive themselves. What was interesting about his comment is that shame and shunning are probably two of the worst things that can happen to a person and to forgive yourself is probably equally as hard. I don't take the action of forgiving myself for my wrongdoings lightly; it is a critical skill that you will continue to use over and over for the remainder of your life.

FEELING AND SEEING THROUGH THE LENS OF OTHERS IS A GREAT SECRET.

When I was young I lived in a trailer park with my mom, aunt, and cousins. My biological dad was nowhere in sight, and I was, for the most part, on my own. Mom had her hands full working full-time, trying to take care of us kids, and everything else. It made me see that if I wanted something, I needed to make it happen. Sometimes, that meant making decisions that people around me didn't understand. While in high school, I had a decent union job bagging groceries.

During my senior year, I decided I would break the mold and be the only one in my family to attend a four-year university. At the beginning of summer, I set my plan in motion. I was going to summon up my courage, quit my union job, and go to college. When I announced it to my family, my aunt was disappointed in me. "I can't believe you're quitting your job to go to college," she said. "That's a good union job, Rod."

At the time, this was hard. I was young and questioned my decision, but I knew I needed to stick to my goal. I couldn't understand why she was saying this. After some time, I came to realize that her care and concern was authentic. I respectfully listened to her and saw that her advice came from a place of love. Ultimately, I ignored it, however, because I knew what I had to do.

People in our lives may seem like they're pulling us down. The trick is to recognize that when people are saying these things, it is THEIR belief, not ours. We don't have to believe them. But right or wrong, we may eventually thank them for their intentions. Dr. Alfred Painter wisely states, "Saying thank you is more than good manners. It is good spirituality."

So, as German theologian Meister Eckhart posited, "If the only prayer you said in your whole life was, 'Thank you,' that would suffice." Taking from Painter's and Eckhart's advice, Auntie, I thank you. Your subconscious motivational speech to a teenaged boy was the speech that would shape my life in ways I never dreamed possible.

Maybe it's not just childhood memories that get us down. Maybe a recently lost job or a spouse deciding to move on will be the kicker. The key is to realize that we're not victims, and we're not failures, either. Think about this: What do you feel when you say that you "failed" at something instead of saying, "That was a consequence I do not want to have again"? If you don't like the result you got from something, figure out what you can do to make it turn out better next time.

My cycling coach used to say, "Being a winner is coming in ninth place when you came in fifteenth place last time." Acknowledging what it is we need to work on, and NEVER calling ourselves failures, is one key to movin' on.

As I said earlier, we are where we are based on a series of experiences that shaped our current beliefs. Will Rogers said, "Judgment comes from experience, and a lot of that comes from bad judgment."

MISTAKES ARE JUST EXPERIENCES
WITH ERROR THAT ALLOW FOR GROWTH.

Everyone makes mistakes, but rather than sitting yourself down in the mistake goo, why not change it into an experience? Lawyer and diplomat Edward John Phelps said it best: "The [person] who makes no mistakes does not usually make anything."

I know I'm starting to sound like a broken record—but which beliefs do you attach to the experiences, good or bad, that occupy your mind? This is an important question, whether you're talking about a small white lie, or an illegal, "you're-going-to-jail" kind of action. Maybe it's a recurring mistake, or maybe it's a one-off. What I do know is that a mistake is something that was driven by a belief, which eventually led to an action.

BECOME HYPER AWARE OF THAT
LITTLE VOICE IN YOUR HEAD.

Let's take this thought to the next level. Become hyper aware of that little voice in your head. What is it saying about your body ... your business practices ... your relationships ... your spirituality ... your various skill sets? For the next day or two, meditate on what beliefs, good or bad, you have spinning in your head. Do not judge or think too much about them. Just see what you discover in your mind.

This may seem like a meaningless task, but I can assure you it is not. For me, it was a most powerful exercise. With every second, your mind is rewiring itself by adapting to the environment in which you presently find yourself, the beliefs you embrace, and the energies you allow in. If you can become aware and inject positive beliefs into all things, your magical, powerful mind will mystically move you toward a wonderful place of contentment. Once you learn how to awaken to awareness, you will have discovered a critical path to movin' on.

CHOOSE AND SET YOUR INTENTIONS CAREFULLY.

The key is not only to become aware of your beliefs, but to embrace the ones that serve you and rewrite the ones that don't. For example, if your counter-thought to the negative belief was, "I am an exerciser and healthy eater," then embrace that thought, anchoring it in your mindset by saying it repeatedly. If you said, "I am poor at managing my spending," you can change that to, "I am so thankful I am a financially wise person." Even if you are not an exerciser or financially wise person, keep saying it anyway. If you take a Saturday off from exercising and eat junk food, say: "I am an exerciser and healthy eater that took Saturday off."

Again, believe you are the belief, allow your self-talk to become the belief, and, in time, you will manifest that belief and find ways to get help from the world around you. Let me say it more clearly: A manifesting statement, repeated over time with conviction and passion, will eventually become your new belief—and the new you.

Most people living in this busy world are deaf to the little voice in their head. But you don't need deep therapy or someone else to tell you what to do ... you need to shut up and listen to that voice in your head! Once you begin to hear it, you can bring in new actors who speak lines from your life script—lines that serve you!

Verbally—I mean out loud—repeat these three statements during your daily meditation for the next three weeks. And if by chance you have a cigarette on a Friday night, do not fret. You are a non-smoker who had one cigarette. You have not failed. Go back to meditating on your intention statements, and, over time, you will become the belief.

Finally, note that the true intention statement happens at a depth where you are truly actualizing that belief. In short, you will know when you have fully anchored this belief, because you'll never think of smoking again.

SOLVING PROBLEMS MINDFULLY.

There is a strategy used by many business leaders and psychologists to get to the root of a problem. Some call it "The four questions that lead to understanding." Most professionals believe that by simply creating and then answering these four questions, one can bring awareness to the root cause of nearly every problem.

Here's how it works: Start with the belief that you have a problem (because it's not really a problem). Let's say, for example, that the problem is you believe your employees are lazy and are not doing their jobs as efficiently as they should. You believe that due to their inefficiencies, the business is losing a lot of money, and you're feeling angry.

THE FOUR QUESTIONS.

The aim of the four questions in this hypothetical situation is to find out what's really behind the problem. Note: It may not be what you think!

Question 1: "Why are the employees not doing a good job?"
Answer: Because they believe they are not getting enough training.
Question 2: "Why are they not getting the training needed to do a good job?"
Answer: Because the manager is too busy running around doing the books and going to corporate meetings instead of training the staff.
Question 3: "Why is the manager not spending time training the staff?"
Answer: Because there isn't a bookkeeper on staff, and he must pay the bills.
Question 4: "Why didn't we hire a bookkeeper?"
Answer: We didn't think we needed one.

MOVIN' ON ACTION

Write down three intention statements in the present tense. For example, if you are trying to quit smoking, you might write the following:

1. I'm a non-smoker.
2. I enjoy breathing clean, fresh air.
3. I'm an example to my kids and/or friends.

1. _____

2. _____

3. _____

MOVIN' ON ACTION

Think of an experience from your past which you believe negatively affects you in the present. Write down how you can forgive yourself for your part in the experience and others for their part? Note: Movin' on is virtually impossible without forgiveness. Let go!

_____

_____

_____

_____

_____

_____

_____

_____

_____

_____

_____

_____

_____

_____

Curious that we spend more time congratulating people who have succeeded than encouraging people who have not."

—*Neil deGrasse Tyson*

Here we can see that the real problem wasn't "lazy" or untrained employees but the lack of a bookkeeper—something the owner had not realized. You can use this method in your own personal assessment. It's an irreverent way of challenging your mindset and current beliefs. Over time, your ability to assess your mindfulness will improve, and you will be surprised at the solutions and ideas that you come up with. Things are rarely as they appear to be. Surprise yourself!

WE ALL HAVE THE OPPORTUNITY TO ADDRESS CHALLENGES AND LEARN FROM THE PAST.

As we embrace our own mindfulness, being kind toward others who are also experiencing grief can be cathartic. In my circle of cyclist friends, we've discussed the diverse opinions and myriad of emotions that surrounded the Lance Armstrong doping scandal. Do we need to go to such lengths to hate and cause further pain? On a spiritual level, everyone deserves a dose of compassion.

The second we start hating on someone or projecting negative energy, the neurons in our minds immediately alter our hormones and change us. There are as many potential connections between neurons in our brain as there are atoms in the universe, so we shouldn't underestimate their power. By controlling our neurons, we control our happiness and our destiny—or, should I say, by chasing happiness we control our neurons?

The next time you are being put down, or are putting someone else down, try to become mindful of how you feel. When you are angry or putting out low vibrations, you are releasing stress hormones. If you choose to be a person who cuts others down or gets angry easily, you are dripping out negative stress-related hormones—and unless you thrive on "Schadenfreude," (finding joy in others' pain), it doesn't feel good!

Being awake enough to know when we are speaking poorly of others is a good thing. I can't think of too many moments in my life where knocking someone down was beneficial. So, if we consciously think on how we are going to build others up and compassionately offer our support to help them, we exert ourselves for our collective good.

It is said that the typical human gravitates toward negative neurons. It's apparently a genetic behavior. Eighty percent of the front-page news of every major paper in the United States is of a negative nature. The truth is, bad news sells papers, and good news doesn't. But, we can change and gravitate toward the positive news instead!

WE ALL KNOW THE BEAUTY THAT RESIDES IN KINDNESS, BUT WHY DO SO MANY PEOPLE STRUGGLE TO BE KIND?

Again, we are one big consciousness, and what happens to others is happening to us. Please consider that if you started believing in this inner connectedness tomorrow, you might approach the day just a little bit differently than you did today. It is sad when people who have made their own fair share of mistakes still find the energy to hurt others with their words or actions.

What if you changed the way you think right now and became a catalyst in the office or at school? What if you became someone who doesn't engage in negative talk toward others, but instead says positive things about whomever the group is knocking down? Over time, you would become the most trusted person. The key is to be consistent; the way to stay consistent is to stay mindful.

For me, finding forgiveness in my heart for those who had hurt me was difficult at first. However, by staying mindful on the quality of my compassionate, forgiving mind, versus focusing on the things that were "going to hurt me and my family," I creatively worked through the pain and confusion. Anyone can do this.

When I hear my cycling friends referring to Lance with words like, "I hope he suffers… let him have it," that makes me hurt. I'm not defending his actions or justifying his behavior. However, when we choose compassion, we help those who are wrong to rise above their misgivings. As opposed to disciplining with jail time, fines, or shunning, compassion and a true commitment to help one become better has proven more effective in some cases. Indeed, the Bible says: "Do not rejoice when your enemy falls, and do not let your heart be glad when he stumbles" (Proverbs 24:17).

Eleanor Roosevelt once asked the question: "When will our conscience grow so tender that we will act to prevent human misery rather than avenge it?"

We all know the beauty that resides in kindness, but why do so many people struggle to be kind? It can be very difficult when dealing with a difficult person. Try this exercise to help you:

MOVIN' ON ACTION

In your next meditation, set your intention on someone you dislike. Then, visualize someone who loves and cares for him or her. Imagine the two of them interacting and allow that experience to settle in your mind. How does this change your perception of that person?

There are far, far
better things
ahead than any we
leave behind

— C.S. LEWIS

GET OUTSIDE OF YOURSELF

If you want others to be happy, practice compassion.
If you want to be happy, practice compassion.

—The Dalai Lama

The great coach, John Wooden, was spot on: "You can't live a perfect day without doing something for someone who will never repay you." I would add that you could do this for animals and the environment, as well. Are you doing this? Can you come to an awareness that is built on preventing misery rather than blindly accepting it—or, worse, causing it? Can you get outside of yourself?

WE ALL HAVE SHORT-TERM MEMORIES.

After completing the Ironman several times, winning many international races, and participating in the Olympic trials twice, my ego learned an important lesson: no one remembers how good you used to be. The good thing is, no one remembers how bad you used to be either. If you or someone you know is working through a personal crisis, remember that there is no one out there sitting around and worrying about you (okay, maybe your mom). I don't mean this in a negative way. If you made the paper for getting a DWI or whatever, it's good to know that most people don't care, and that other than a few conversations and gossip at the office, it will go away. The ancient poets said it clearly: "This too shall pass."

IF WE WANT TO CHANGE OUR BEHAVIOR,
WE NEED TO CHANGE OUR BELIEFS.

Getting outside of ourselves is difficult when we are in pain. Think of it

---
MOVIN' ON ACTION

To do this gently and creatively, bring your mind back from those spinning thoughts and instead cultivate compassion, fearlessness, humility, and gratitude. In other words, in your meditative space, deliberately train your mind to say and truly believe that:

1. I possess compassion, humility, joy, and appreciation...
2. No action, good or bad, can define who I am...
3. I don't have a problem owning my own mistakes...
4. If others do, that's their problem...
5. If my mind wanders, I can mindfully bring it back to No. 1.

like a reverse ego. How we deal with this is our issue. If we are struggling with how others think about us, we are their prisoner. To free yourself from this problem, you can use the creative meditation technique. Creative meditation is the same as regular focused meditation, but it is used to strengthen specific types of qualities of mind. In the case of a DWI incident (or some other thing, large or small, which may have gotten others talking), your mind may have a tendency to wander away and ruminate on what others think.

We can get out of this prison and creatively strengthen the quality of our minds. We all know that behavior can shape our reputation. If we want to change our behavior, we first need to change our beliefs.

Doing this MOA will create a new pathway in your mind. In the future, when you hear others gossiping about you, your mind will go on autopilot and say something like, "I'm sorry they feel that way, but I know differently." Don't forget the power of the unconscious. Your highly trained mind will move toward what it believes—it will direct your physical body away from toxic people and their off-putting energies. It will squash any negativity that has the potential to create pathways that will not serve you. Moreover, it will shelter your ears and eyes from the words of others, so those actions cannot anchor in your mind. It will be a mental shield that protects you from the negative energy, and it will be an energetic field that encourages new thoughts and beliefs in those around you. Eventually, almost everyone will stop talking. Then you can face the harder challenge of convincing yourself that this is you, in perpetuity.

We'll go over this in future chapters, but for now, just remember your "Big Mistake," when combined with a consciousness designed to change your beliefs, will soon mean very little to anyone—including you!

Sometimes "real" psychological issues are hard to separate from perceived crabbiness or a temporary unhappy quality of mind. I have a friend who is in the flower business. Once, she was hired by a wealthy woman to create two outdoor winter arrangements for $600. Due to minimal orders and the idea that she would create more for other clients, she ordered $1,000 worth of supplies. She planned on using one third of these supplies for the outdoor winter arrangement. Dressed for winter, she arrived at the client's house on time, brought all the supplies into the garage, and was about to begin creating the arrangement when the woman came running out of the house and screamed at her maniacally: "You're worthless! Is this all you have? Do you think I am going to pay you $600 for just this little project? Get off my property!"

My friend was in shock. She didn't know what to say. The client had already paid her the $600, but there was $1,000 worth of supplies in the garage. My friend wisely said to herself, "Okay, I realize this isn't about me."

She told the woman, "I will give you your $600 back. Please let me back into the garage so I can get my supplies, and I will leave."

The woman refused to let her back in saying, "Keep your money, and leave!"

My friend said, "I am not going to leave until you open the garage door and let me take my supplies." Again, she told herself, "This is not about me, it's about her."

After five minutes, the woman, who was obviously dealing with other issues, broke down and said, "Fine, just do the project then." To avoid an unpleasant confrontation, my friend reluctantly did the arrangement.

"That is so beautiful," the woman said at last.

> **Eternity is not the hereafter. Eternity has nothing to do with time. This is it. If you don't get it here, you won't get it anywhere. The experience of eternity right here and now is the function of life. Heaven is not the place to have the experience; here's the place to have the experience."**
>
> *—Joseph Campbell*

Her husband came home, and remarked, "That is the most beautiful arrangement we have ever had, I hope it finally makes my wife happy."

My friend felt much better, and, as she was about to leave, the client handed her another check with tears in her eyes, and said, "Can you make me two more?" My friend smiled and kindly declined.

Having the ability to discern someone's dysfunction from simply "having a bad day" is another skill for movin' on. It's your life, and you can walk away from most things you encounter in it. Find the courage to be mindful of how you do it.

BY STAYING PRESENT, WE CAN UNDO THE CHAINS THAT SHACKLE US TO THE PAST.

We've all heard it before: the key to a life filled with contentment is to stay present, allowing all experiences to come and go effortlessly. We can become aware of the debilitating beliefs that are creating anxiety about our future. Even if awful things happened to us in the past, we can create new beliefs so that we don't continue to own those things in our present or future. Physicists say there is no such thing as time. If that is true, then we can—right now—change how past relationships unfolded. I know that sounds weird, and it may be difficult to comprehend, but we tend to approach life linearly, when, in metaphysical terms, it's not.

MOVIN' ON ACTION

In your next meditation, explore your various friends' mindsets, and write down which ones serve your joy, and which ones challenge it.

_____

_____

_____

_____

_____

_____

_____

_____

_____

_____

_____

_____

_____

_____

_____

_____

_____

_____

Show me your friends and I will show you your future."

—*John Kuebler*

WHOM WE HANG OUT WITH SHAPES WHO WE ARE.

I had a colleague who regularly badmouthed his girlfriend, complained about his blue-collar job, and told inappropriate racist jokes. We had known each other for years. After several months of mindfulness training, I consciously decided to limit how much I hung out with him. A year later, I could honestly see some new, subtle changes in my life.

We don't really know how our trillion neurons will react to the things we do in our lives, but I can assure you that if you are exchanging the negatives for the positives that life offers, you will go in the right direction. Breaking free from those who are not feeding us isn't always easy. However, the good news is, we can still maintain a friendship; we just need to set healthy boundaries. You can even take this to the next level and set an intention that helps your friend become their best self. Reflecting on my own life, I have found that being with true, authentic friends that feed me has been my rock.

Mastery is our ability to discover what's feeding both us and those around us. Maybe you'll feel compelled to share with them what you learned from this next exploration.

Several years ago, a dear friend of mine went through a bad divorce. He suffered depression from a broken heart. Sometimes he felt like it was too hard to go on.

He was in one of those situations where it's very difficult to change your thinking. The pain was so great that simply getting through the day was all he could think of. To overcome this debilitating pattern, I gently asked him to focus on being present: "What is going on right now?" At that particular moment, he was with his dog, having a cup of tea with me, and telling stories. Right now, that was all he had—all he could know.

MOVIN' ON ACTION

One way to better understand who's enhancing your life is to create and keep a script journal. A script journal is a playful way to explore your story and all actors who play a role in it.

Here's how:

On a piece of paper, write down your current life story as though you were presenting it to Hollywood executives. Who are the actors and co-stars in your movie? How do these others act in your movie? How does a typical day, week, or month with all these people play out? After writing this down—honestly and without judgment—pretend you are presenting it to the person you respect most in your life. How do you feel when you share this script with that person?

Now ask yourself, "How do I want to feel? How do I want others to feel?" When people are important in your life, what they feel about you matters.

If you need to write a new script to match those new feelings, write it now. Make sure you write it in the forward-thinking, present-tense narrative that describes your new life and the new you. Now present this script—with the chosen, real-life co-stars and actors who synergistically co-create a story you are proud of—to the person you respect the most. How does it feel? Does it feel different? Does it feel more positive?

Now, do not just let this be another meaningless exercise. You need to become that person, even if you must "act" at first. "Fake it until you make it," as the old saying goes.

LET SAD THINGS MAKE YOU SAD.
JUST DON'T HANG OUT IN SADNESS.

Over time, he successfully trained his mind to be in the moment. Instead of worrying and creating false stories about what the future would look like, he focused on the here-and-now. This very conscious decision to stay in the moment changed his thinking, and today, he is with another great woman, lives life to the fullest, and seems truly content.

If we're in a negative place and leave our consciousness to chance, we'll rarely succeed, because our brain will try to find a way to pull us down. Developing a positive belief system based on a mind that is searching for happiness is both difficult and rewarding. It will come as no surprise that my friend had to shift his awareness from thinking about what he "lost" toward thinking in the present moment. He did this by meditating. If you've learned one thing so far in this book, I hope it is that connecting awareness to action can create wonders.

SET AN INTENTION AND CONSISTENTLY
MOVE TOWARD IT.

What do you think the difference is between prayer and meditation? Really think about it. Why would you pray? Why would you meditate? There's no one answer, but some say that prayer is asking for something or being grateful for something, while meditating carries no expectation.

You may have heard from others that you need to "set an intention." The question is, what does this practically look like? How do we really do this? Setting an effective intention is having the ability to convert words into energy.

Because the present is fluid and moves ever forward, staying on top of our intention of joy is a continuous practice. After setting our first intention, we may quickly experience certain benefits. In short order, we may find ourselves not fighting with our co-workers, not arguing with our spouse, or not reacting badly to rough patches in our lives. In other words, our new intention will instantly replace actions that once led to misery with actions or responses that lead to new levels of joy. In time, we may need to tweak our intention and deepen our practice to continue to experience such benefits in our lives. It's not a one-time deal, and it may seem awkward, at first, to think that by changing our intentions we change what happens to us. Isn't it fun to know that the things we think are set in stone are not always as they appear? Want to know how to break the stone?

MOVIN' ON ACTION

Let's say your new purpose is to find joy. First, calm your mind with a moving or seated meditation. Once your mind is quiet, set your intention to find joy. Simply say, "I'm thankful that I am moving toward joy in all that I do in the coming present moments." How does that feel? What actions arise from that awareness?

_____

_____

_____

_____

_____

_____

_____

_____

_____

_____

_____

_____

HOW TO SET AN EFFECTIVE INTENTION
STATEMENT FOR A SPECIFIC GOAL:

Think of something you would really like to do but somehow can't find the energy and discipline for. It is very important that this "something" is a harmonious goal. For example, let's say you want to learn how to play the piano. The first step is that you need to be able to see yourself at the finish line. In this particular example, you need to see yourself playing the piano well. The second step is that you need to attach emotion to you playing the piano. For example, maybe you see yourself playing during the holidays, while everyone gathers around the piano singing and laughing.

Now that you've attached a mindful emotion to playing the piano, set your intention on hiring a teacher, or set time aside daily to follow a "Learn to Play Piano" YouTube channel. If you can believe it, you can achieve it. You will find yourself enjoying the piano lessons, practicing daily, and, if you keep the emotional intensity at a high level, you will become as accomplished as you believed you would. Remember the adage: Whether you think you can or think you can't, you are right.

IF WE BELIEVE IT, WE CAN ACHIEVE IT.

My colleague, Erin, shared with me a question that her friend, Elizabeth, had asked her.

Elizabeth: "Hey Erin, do you know why no one has ever seen a sunset?"

Erin: "What do you mean? I've seen hundreds of sunsets!"

Elizabeth: "I used to think the same, but actually you are not watching a sunset, you are witnessing the beauty of the earth turning."

Being wise as you frame intentions is a prerequisite to happiness. Think about one of the most famous prayers, The Serenity Prayer:

God, grant me the serenity to accept the things
I cannot change, the courage to change the
things I can, and the wisdom to know the difference.

Do you believe this can be true? Go back and reread this prayer, and really try to make sense of it.

With that said, here's the paradox: Everything changes. think about it for a minute. Maybe you are short and cannot change that. But, what if you were to change your perception of what is short? You may have heard that perception is reality. In other words, you can only change yourself, your perceptions, and your relationships—with yourself, with others, and with situations. We cannot change other people, only our actions toward them. The big question is: Are you willing to honor the fact that perception has the power to make change in ourselves, and in others, in ways that we are sometimes perhaps too narrow-minded to understand?

— MOVIN' ON ACTION —

Can you really accept the things you cannot change? What are those things? Do you truly have the courage to change the things that you can change? What are those things? Do you truly know the difference?

Write down 3 things you can change right now:

1. _____

2. _____

3. _____

Write down 3 things you cannot change:

1. _____

2. _____

3. _____

PERCEPTION IS REALITY.

I had a buddy who was going through a tough breakup with his girl-friend. His belief was that life was miserable, and that he was being dumped on by the universe. He was a Christian, and thought medita-tion was for Buddhists. I asked him to think about the difference between prayer and meditation, and how intention statements might relate to that difference. I kept on him every time we saw one another. "Pray for the awareness that you can move toward being present," I would say.

He began to see what that meant, in practical terms. "I'm walking my dog in the woods, and this crazy squirrel is screaming at us. What is this critter trying to tell me?" He started to feel that the value of being present was more playful, that being in the moment was much more fun than wallowing in self-pity.

Regardless of his newfound mindfulness training, his ex-girlfriend would still say hurtful things that would catch him off-guard. She would insinuate that he was a lousy boyfriend, or that he wasn't good enough for her. I encouraged him to be careful not to become those beliefs, but to be mindful of his reaction.

He shared with me his profound response to her comment about him being a terrible boyfriend: "I'm sorry you feel that way; I know differently." He was beginning to retrain his brain, and it was exciting! He continues to learn how to respond positively to her and others. He is creating new neurological pathways—and new beliefs. We all have the ability do this!

OUR MIND IS OUR BEST FRIEND.
BUT WHY DOES OUR BRAIN TELL US DUMB THINGS?

If you are walking down the street, and a stranger says, "That outfit looks terrible on you," you might be offended—but most likely, you would think that that person was just a jerk and then move on. However, if our significant other says it, that could really hurt. Our mind can be the same way. It has the power to make us believe that we're obese, a loser, scared, socially weak, and so on.

Have you ever given thought to how or why your brain is saying those things? After all, it's not like you're just sitting there thinking, "Gee, it's been a few minutes, and now it's time for my brain to knock me down a couple of notches. Go brain!"

I can assure you, you are not alone, and these unwelcome thoughts most likely come from emotionally powerful experiences (good or bad) from your past. Such thoughts are there to protect us from something. They are telling us what, who, and how we should be. The brain puts in a lot of effort to "protect" us. The good news is, regardless of whether these thoughts are based on old childhood beliefs, an event that happened last week, or years of self-sabotage, we can change the way we think. The secret is to be awake enough to catch the thought in the first place and, then, to ask ourselves if that thought serves us. Mindfulness exercises bring these questions to the surface, so we can deal with them in our conscious mind.

There is no right or wrong way to do these mindfulness exercises. Simply put on the catcher's mitt in your head, and, when a thought comes up that doesn't serve you, toss it back to the pitcher (the universe). For example, if a thought arises telling you to avoid talking to your spouse about something that's bothering you—because the last time you did an angry fight ensued—reframe that thought. Reframe it so that you are not going to avoid the conversation, but, instead, focus on how you are going to change your communication approach to avoid a fight.

Training your mind actively can be done in a way that is fun, practical, and effective. By following a daily mind/body practice, you can train your mind to handle anything that might possibly come up.

THE DAILY MIND/BODY CONTINUUM PRACTICE.

The following is a daily routine to strengthen your mind and control your brain:

1. Create success.

After you wake up, immediately make your bed. This may seem like a small thing, but the very act of doing something successfully, and mindfully recognizing this success, however small, triggers your brain's success neurons. Eventually, you will begin to find other actions throughout the day, large and small, that resulted from your brain easily accessing the success neurons, giving you results. And all you had to do to get it started was to make your bed!

2. Re-tune your body.

Every joint in your body can either help or hinder your body's flow of energy. By rotating the joints, you "snap" them into place like plugging two extension cords together, enhancing the flow of energy. Do the following routine every morning, and you will feel absolutely great:

a. Warm up by doing four deep squats with legs shoulder-width apart, and four with your legs together.

b. Do four deep lunges on each leg (Tip: Don't let your knees go over your toes).

c. Then, standing on your right leg, rotate your left ankle by drawing the alphabet with your big toe (A-M), switch feet, and draw N-Z with the right big toe. Feel the ankles cracking into place.

d. With your knees bent, put your hands on your knees, and rotate the knees side-to-side and circle around. Visualize yourself downhill skiing as you go side-to-side. Feel the rush?

e. Put your hands on your hips and circle five times around to the right, and five times around to the left, opening your lower back and hips.

f. Put your hands on the small of your lower back, bring your chin to your chest, and gently press your hips forward ten times in a pulsing motion. This will aid, again, in opening your lower back and hips.

g. Lifting your right hand high in the air, lean over as far as you can to the left, forming a large letter C with your body. Gently pulse ten times. Switch sides.

h. Bend your arms ninety degrees and do a bent arm backstroke ten times on each side by making large circles backwards. Reverse the movement and do large circles forward. Again, any cracking you hear is from your shoulder joints falling into place, leading to better flow of energy.

i. Rotate your head in large circles, ten times to the right and ten times to the left, opening the cervical spine.

j. Rotate your elbows, wrists, and fingers—again "cracking" them into proper joint placement.

3. Cultivate gratitude.

Before eating breakfast, write down or speak aloud three things you are thankful for. This may happen as a form of prayer before you eat, or just a simple action. By doing this, you will trigger the part of your brain that oversees gratitude, positioning you for a day of living with a thankful attitude. In short order, others will find you very attractive and will want to be around you. Remember not only to give gratitude for the things you have in your life, but for people, energy, and a mind that is willing to push you toward harmonious living.

4. Embrace your inner wisdom.

During breakfast, avoid reading news of a negative nature. (Don't look at the newspaper!). Instead, read something philosophical. This will awaken the deep-thinking portion of your brain. The goal is to read something that will make you ponder a thought or an idea. In time, you will find yourself coming up with creative solutions to problems that were otherwise difficult to solve.

5. Get things done.

Now, go to work. This is the time to train your brain to get busy "working." If it is allowed, now is the time to read the journals of your trade, watch the daily news, or just to catch up on details of life. It is critical that you do not get buried in your "devices," or other technological things, other than what you need to get your job done. Use discipline to avoid social media and other things that keep you from being productive. Set an intention that you will catch up on your Facebook, Twitter, Instagram, or other "important" things at lunchtime, and again after work. This will trigger your brain's productivity area, and, by delaying gratification of social media or other such detractors, you will train the discipline and functional work portions of your brain. Consciously, keep humor and playfulness in the forefront of your newfound discipline. It will help you with your creative processes

6. Exercise and connect to nature.

Before or after work, find the time to exercise for 30–60 minutes—preferably outdoors and in nature. Mix in 20–50 minutes of cardio (jog or bike), 10–30 minutes of strength training (core exercises, like push-ups and plank or weight training), and 5–10 minutes of flexibility exercises (stretches or yoga). No matter what, do something! Exercise, repeated daily, will re-tune that little voice in your brain that may be keeping you from developing healthy exercise behaviors. Again, even just walk for thirty minutes in your work clothes after work and do a few wall push-ups and hand-to-toe stretches. You do not need to go to the gym every day or do some super-serious workout. However, it is absolutely important that you do something. Remember, the things you repeat regularly form new neural pathways, which eventually form new habits. It is said that it takes three weeks to form a habit. See if you can make it happen in less! Habits, once formed, require very little discipline to make happen. Control and form good ones.

7. Be playful.

After you've finished exercising and have eaten a healthy supper, play board games with your family, do a crossword puzzle, or catch up on your fun reading. You can even watch meaningless TV shows. Just find the time to be with that part of the brain that wants to mix thinking with play and relaxation.

8. Anchor meaningful thoughts before bedtime.

After 9 p.m., turn off the news or any reading that is charged or emotional. Instead, read a biography about someone you respect, or listen to easy music. The goal is to slow your brain and allow emotions to simmer down. By reading a biography, you will fall asleep with those thoughts in your head. The words of someone you respect and want to emulate will, in time, rewire your brain to anchor ideals subconsciously, in your sleep, which will serve you when you're awake. Again, turn off all TV and computer screens. Research has shown that the light emulating from a computer screen wakes your brain up like caffeine.

As I mentioned previously, what you do repeatedly will train your brain's neurons. What's important is that you train your mind to tell your brain what you want to do. By living out meaningful and fun behaviors, you will trigger areas of the brain in ways that lead to a life of purpose and meaning.

Dr. Bruce Lipton has theorized that repeated behaviors can literally change your DNA (Google "epigenetics" to learn more). Make a conscious choice to change these behaviors in ways that serve you and your future children. In short, it doesn't matter whether you make your bed, or finish a book, or do a crossword puzzle, or play a game. What matters is that you mindfully, with full awareness, do something that triggers those various areas of your brain that might be filled with cobwebs.

When we follow The Daily Mind/Body Continuum Practice regularly, we subconsciously strengthen the areas of the brain that lead to a successful and holistic life. While this may be just a template for taking charge of your brain, it is a good first step. Now, keep on movin' on!

KEEP SMILING.

A psychologist friend once told me that there are more than eighty pressure points in your face that get compressed when you smile. When these points are pressed, they release endorphins, or happy hormones. As we know, smiling is infectious. Others feel our happiness when we smile. The crow's feet around our eyes that result from a lifetime of smiling become permanent wrinkles—a tattoo telling everyone looking at us that we are happy people. People love being around happy people. Smiling, even if we are faking it, will help us navigate through problems. Don't Botox these beautiful wrinkles away! They are proof of happiness and joy in your life.

THE MAGIC OF A SMILE.

I remember getting lost in the woods with my friend, Randy, an avid outdoorsman. We were bird hunting, and, after four hours of searching for birds deep in the northern Minnesota woods, we decided to leave.

"Let's go this way," I said.

He replied, "No, we need to go this way."

We were lost. We could have become scared and panicked, but we didn't. Instead, we looked at each other and started laughing. An outdoor education director, he said with a chuckle, "If our students could see us now!" Eventually we found our way out of the woods and realized that by smiling and finding humor in the situation, we had more readily overcome adversity.

When it comes to challenges, a narrow world-view tells us that we need to have the power to push through problems, to have the strength to overcome them. However, a wider world-view encourages us to embrace challenges. Let me ask you this: What if you were to see a challenge as something to be embraced, instead of something you needed to muscle your way through? What if you were to respond to a challenge as an invitation to look within, to see what's there, rather than as something that causes you pain?

I know a woman who encountered a challenge she believed would confront her for the rest of her life. At the age of two, her daughter passed away following a surgical repair to her congenitally damaged heart. For months, she wrestled with her anguish, anger, and hopelessness, and she and her husband could not even grieve together. It somehow seemed that doing so might completely break one or the other.

Many caring people tried to ease the pain, but their sentiments only served to make it worse. Things like, "God needed her in Heaven," or "You still have three other children," or "You can still have more children," did nothing to ease the heartache. This woman spent a full year going to the cemetery once a week to sit with her child and wonder what had gone wrong – and what SHE had done to deserve this.

Eventually, she made the conscious decision that she could not go on living her life this way. It wasn't serving her, and it certainly wasn't serving the rest of her family. She began to study and research everything she could find about coping with the loss of a child—what her faith said, what others in the same situation said, what every book said.

This decision to learn and explore the workings of the human body, her own mind, and the workings of her faith changed her life completely. She finally accepted that her daughter's death was not something she could have changed and was no one's fault. It was the result of the way humans are made: imperfect. And it was not something she needed to "battle" for the rest of her life. She could instead rejoice that her daughter was in God's care and that she would see her again one day. She could move on toward being the best mom, wife, teacher, and friend she could be. Seeing the challenge as an invitation to "look within" saved her from a life of despair and enabled her to grow in many ways.

WE TEACH PEOPLE HOW TO TREAT US.

What happens outside of ourselves reflects our inner landscape. We teach people how to treat us. If we don't like what is happening "to us," we need to become aware of what is going on inside us. Becoming aware of this will change the way we approach everything in our lives. This is arguably the most powerful movin' on concept in this whole book. How we manicure our inner landscape is the secret to a life filled with joy. To better understand this, we need to search inward to find out what is leading others to respond to us as they do. Meditation is one process for this discovery.

Once you've written down these things, just sit with them. Can you bring awareness to these behaviors and form new actions?

This is a very humbling mindfulness exercise, and you may need to practice self-compassion so as not to lower your self-esteem. If done authentically and without judgment, you will discover traits and behaviors that are affecting your friendships. Remember, your inner landscape is your inner landscape, and no one else's. As you wake up to this inner landscape in a humble way, making change can happen. Once you've done this, you will begin to see your friendships improve and relationships become richer and more meaningful.

MOVIN' ON ACTION

In your next mindful meditation, think of someone you believe finds you irritating or doesn't like you. Explore your inner landscape, and write down any words, body-language postures, tone of voice, or other behaviors that you may be displaying to cause this dislike. If this is difficult, perhaps you can even find the courage to ask the person to be forthright and share what it is about you that irritates them.

WHAT BRINGS US JOY?

The Master's power is this; he lets all things come and go effortlessly, without desire. He never expects results, thus he is never disappointed.

—Lao-Tzu

Do we really want things, or do we want the feeling we think those things will bring us?

After years of personally coaching people, I'm convinced that most folks really do not know what they want. Quite often, their goals and ambitions are driven by the external (i.e., social media, magazines, ads, and TV shows). I often ask: Are folks aware that the fitness models they see on TV and in magazines are the way they are due to severe dieting and/or photo alteration? Many of Hollywood's rich people often lack true, authentic connections to friends and to their communities. Don't be fooled by this media illusion.

An old mentor of mine once asked me, "Do you really want a big house? Or do you want the feelings you think that large house will bring you?" Most folks with big houses probably spend most of their time in just one or two rooms. Further, it's a pain in the neck to maintain and pay for a large house. Maybe we think we want the big boat. Truth is, we want the feelings we think the boat will give us. After all, it's a hassle to take care of, we may only use it a few times a summer, and the cost of storage, maintenance, and running it are high. It is such a relief to know that we are enough, and we already have exactly what we need. How can it be that people in cultures that believe they are enough and have enough are so happy? Is keeping up with Joneses really such a good thing? More to the point, are you living this way?

I am not suggesting it's wrong to have nice things. I have lots of nice things myself. I own an amazing, crazy-expensive bike, which I use and love. I exhilarate in the feeling that my high-end bike gives me. It handles well around corners, climbs hills easily due to its light frame, and shifts gears impeccably. If you own something that truly brings you happiness beyond your ego, then rock on. But what if I didn't have that bike? Could I still be content?

Wisdom is understanding when we are experiencing relative happiness or absolute happiness. Relative happiness, for example, is when one has all the trappings of what appears on the outside to be wonderful: financial security, good relationships, satisfying work, perfect health. It is the kind of happiness we see famous actors and superstar athletes flaunting. On the outside, it seems that these people have everything, but if we looked deeper, we may discover an anxiousness surrounding this happiness, especially if it was achieved based on looks or talent.

In contrast, absolute happiness is the kind of happiness where one develops a state of being in which one is never defeated by the obstacles life throws out, where one feels great joy no matter how much money is coming in or what might be happening in one's environment. We may gain this type of satisfaction only when we develop an interminable joy by living consistently in alignment with our life's purpose. I'm hoping that the Movin' On Actions in my book contribute in some way to your absolute happiness.

In the end, this new awareness, when combined with action or inaction, may serve you up a delicious dose of life-fulfilling contentment.

Erin DeWitt, a professional healer, shared the following wisdom with me:

When is contentment just a state of being with the present? Could contentment simply be feeling complete and content with the unknown? At what point do we recognize that the journey and the present moment are one and the same? If the journey and present moment are the same, then perhaps there would be less of a desire for achievement. From this lens, we could hold an inner wisdom that views everything as perfect. In short, we embody infinite "achievement." We have everything we need in the present moment available to us now—infinite wisdom, happiness, and joy. In knowing this, we would find ourselves truly aligned with contentment that is always evolving and shifting with our experiences and perceptions.

BE HUMBLE.

According to Biblical scholar Matthew George Easton, contentment "arises from the inward disposition, and is the offspring of humility, and of an intelligent consideration of the rectitude and benignity of divine providence."

Serbian forestry scholar Dr. Milosh Ivkovich said after witnessing strife in the former Yugoslavia and traveling around the globe, "There is only one human trait that can impress me at this point in humanity's history: that of humility. Everything else has been overdone."

In other words, joy comes from within the person who is humble and that humility comes from the idea that that there is a higher power (or higher energy) other than ourselves.

MOVIN' ON ACTION

In your next reflective meditation, think about what you have, what you want, and the qualities you want to embrace as a person. No need to pretend—you know when you have put things before people, and consumption before true joy. A question to ponder: "How little do I need to be happy?"

_____

_____

_____

_____

_____

_____

HOW MUCH SPACE IS THERE BETWEEN CONTENTMENT AND HAPPINESS?

The happiness emotion vibrates at a very high level and is impossible to sustain. Can you imagine being in a state of constant elation? You would be dead tired after just a few hours! Instead of trying to be constantly happy, it's okay to seek the middle ground of contentment in our day-to-day, moment-by-moment lives. In today's fast-paced world, being aware of what brings us contentment, and purposefully living to keep content, is incredibly rewarding. We can think of happiness as a "peak" experience that we may feel in the moment, and contentment as a low-level hum when we are satisfied. However, the two are connected. If we consciously nurture contentment in certain areas of life, we will be positioned to enjoy those authentic moments of happiness when they do occur.

For example, if we are content in our job and knock an important presentation out of the park, we will be happy in that moment. If we are satisfied with our child, and she gives a funny performance in the school play, we will feel great joy. If we are at peace with our body and run a five-kilometer race in a personal best time, we will feel a depth of happiness that will resonate at a high level. Most people are aware that the kind of happiness that is derived from a single experience wanes in short order. We are only as happy as the current event in our life, even if we already have a base of contentment. Consciously moving toward contentment is not that difficult, and with just some conscientious tweaks to our awareness, we can be in the space to experience ultimate bliss and joy.

This is such an important concept, so let's take it a little further. Imagine you hate your job but still did well on your presentation. Considering that you started out at such a low emotional level (i.e., hating your job), doing well on the presentation perhaps did little to help you feel much happiness.

Even unrelated experiences, left unchecked, can affect your happiness. For example, your girlfriend or boyfriend just dumped you, and that same day at work you are named employee-of-the-year. You barely crack a smile. Due to your current level of contentment, happiness is now a distant planet.

In short, if you are not content with your job, your relationships, your body, your house, your kids—whatever—you need to act to either change your beliefs or change your circumstances (which leads to changed be-

MOVIN' ON ACTION

Rather than focus on what you want, try focusing on what brings you joy. Here's how. Sit back in a comfortable chair, in an upright posture. Take a few deep breaths and smile. Allow the smile to bring positive emotions to your inner landscape. Once you feel relaxed and in the moment, simply begin to explore what brings you joy. Write down what images pop up, what thoughts arise, and what feelings emerge.

_____

_____

_____

_____

_____

_____

_____

_____

_____

_____

_____

_____

_____

_____

You know you are happy if you accidentally break a jar on your kitchen floor, and it's just a minor inconvenience."

—*Glenn Tobey*

liefs). The choice to be content is yours. However, I caution you to be mindful of what is truly a reality playing out in your life and what may be a construct of your imagination.

BALANCE: THE HARMONY BETWEEN ACHIEVEMENT AND FULFILLMENT.

Finding that healthy balance between paying our bills, getting our kids to school on time, cleaning out the gutters (achievement), and going for a walk, taking the time to smell the flowers in our garden, and really listening to children play (fulfillment) can be an ongoing juggling act. If we live our lives solely for fulfillment but ignore that car loan payment, they'll come and take our car away. Alternatively, if we live our life solely for achievement, we'll miss the sunset or our child's soccer game. Finding the balance requires the cultivation of wisdom. In other words, I believe when you achieve a sweet blend in your daily life between fulfillment and achievement, you've reached genuine contentment. If we find balance, we'll find wisdom.

Finding balance may not equate to quitting your job tomorrow or spending four hours at the beach waiting for the sunset. But changing your beliefs can change your life and how you experience joy and work. Perhaps you will begin to experience a sunset with both your eyes and your ears, or perhaps that child's laughter will speak to you in ways that remind you of your toddler years. What if the two dogs playing at the park truly bring about a playfulness in you that's been dormant for years? What if paying your bills on time feels good? Could it be that finishing that home-improvement project yields a level of satisfaction that carries a sense of meaning greater than the project itself? What would your life look like if you were able to change your attitude about how you see achievement and fulfillment?

Rarely do we hear of a ninety-year-old wishing he'd spent more time at work, or of an underachiever declaring himself glad he never brought his great idea to the marketplace.

MOVIN' ON ACTION

After meditating, explore what you are seeking in terms of career, home, and personal possessions, and compare it to what you are seeking in your community, family, and nature. Invite any threats, opportunities, or irreverent thoughts you may have to enter this meditation. Write down what comes to mind and what your intuition suggests that you do.

_____

_____

_____

_____

_____

_____

_____

_____

_____

_____

_____

WE ARE FLAWED IN OUR PERFECTION!

Do you take the time to appreciate you? This is tough for most folks. In cognitive therapy, the therapist often allows the person to say what is going badly in their life, and then tries to get them to reframe and say what is going well.

They may say, "I'm a bad person because I shut the elevator on a person hurrying to get on."

The therapist may agree that this was bad, but then asks, "What did you do well today?"

And the patient may say, "I helped my son with his homework."

ACCEPT YOURSELF WITHOUT JUDGMENT.

While this has merit, another approach to gaining self-love could be to teach ourselves to be more self-aware. Instead of focusing on our actions and letting them determine our self-worth, we could take a step back. Remember, we are not our thoughts. A person may say they are a bad person and that they don't like themselves. The mindful answer would be, "You are having the thought that you are a bad person. What do you want to do with that thought?"

Self-awareness is not the same as self-compassion. Having self-compassion is going easy on yourself and accepting yourself without judgment. A person with high self-compassion makes room for developing high self-esteem.

If we go easy on ourselves, our creative self can grow. Once the creative self is free, esteem can manifest as much as is needed, and we understand that limits are just that—limits. Additionally, if our esteem is high, our minds cannot be convinced, by ourselves or anyone else, that we are not good enough. Our high-esteem mind knows one thing: become what you are meant to become. Our high-self-compassion mind also knows one thing: Go easy on yourself, as you become the person you are meant to become. Self-awareness, on the other hand, is simply being aware of our thoughts and actions. If we do not inject compassion, our self-aware minds may become abusive.

WE ARE PERFECTLY FLAWED HUMAN BEINGS.

Accepting to be a conscious being in this world takes steady determination, and sometimes we may do or say things that aren't morally or ethically okay. Through our contemplative practice, we can do whatever we wish with the debilitating thoughts that lead to such actions/words. Learning how to be okay with our "flawed" self is okay. It's also okay to grow toward being a more perfectly flawed human being. It's a process—a journey—that continues throughout our lives. Remember, we never totally arrive. To do so would mean that we are "superhuman."

MOVIN' ON: BREAKING FREE FROM OVEREATING.

RYAN BLANCK: My dear friend, Ryan Blanck, used to be extreme-

ly overweight. As the owner of Deviate Consulting, in Nashville, Tennessee, today Ryan is a highly sought-after consultant, speaker, and professional coach. He ended up not only losing weight and getting in shape, but he used the same approach he used to lose weight to start his company and meet the woman of his dreams. Here, he tells us how he did it.

When I was 16 years old, I weighed 245 pounds, which is about a hundred pounds overweight for my height. I lived in Michigan, and over the summer, I was working construction. My friend's grandma, originally from Texas, made these amazing Mexican meals, and we would eat like there was no tomorrow.

One night my buddy called me: "Dinner's on." I totally forgot what I was doing, and I ate so much food—we're talking fifteen tacos, seven tostadas, may have eaten as much as 10,000 calories. I remember laying in the family room on the floor in the fetal position in extreme pain. I was thinking, "What are you doing?"

Then, that same evening, I went and saw another one of my buddies, and had dinner again. He cajoled me, saying, "They've got these new specials. You've gotta try them." I finished what they could not eat as well.

I went home, looked in the mirror and thought, "What are you doing to yourself?"

Shame is a big thing, and it served as a powerful catalyst for wanting to transform. My self-confidence was low, and I was questioning myself. I put on some shoes and limped through a mile. I wasn't happy with who I was, and I was going to do something about it. I didn't know much about nutrition, so I just moved. A best friend introduced me to the gym, and we began to work out together. Once I started to move and could see things changing, my confidence grew.

I had to believe in myself, and then others began to believe in me, too. It took me two years to lose the weight, and I went four years without any sweets. Later, my grandma made homemade cookies, and I'd allow myself to have one rather than six. I lost sixty pounds ... and I've maintained that weight loss since 1996.

Ryan didn't know it at the time, but the decision to get movin' on with his weight-loss goals would end up transforming his life. His newfound mindfulness led him to become a nationally influential leader, speaker, and trainer. One small change with powerful results—that's truly movin' on!

If you want to gain health rather than merely lose weight, then recognize that you need to change your beliefs. Meditate on your new beliefs about health and exercise. Remember your affirmations and intention statements and focus on the person you want to be in a present voice.

Before you know it, your neurons will retrain your mind to see fruits and vegetables rather than junk food, your ears will hear laughter instead of stressful chatter, and your body will become attracted to endorphins racing through it as you and your friends enjoy exercising together.

Let's say you are really struggling with being overweight, and you want to get in shape. The more you think about it, the more you realize that

── **MOVIN' ON ACTION** ──

Be thankful that you are a healthy person who chooses healthy foods, loves to exercise daily, and finds relaxation from stretching. Again, put yourself in the moving present, even if you are not there now. Write down two health-related actions that you can take today.

1. _____

_____

2. _____

_____

Now that you know the "what," write down the "how" for the two actions.

1. _____

_____

2. _____

_____

your weight is affecting your self-image, your relationships, and your mood. Are you going to go on letting your brain believe that you can't change?

Write down what that inner voice is saying and what your mind's eye is seeing. For example, maybe your voice is saying, "I am stressed after a long day at work, and I need something greasy to make me feel better." Your mind's eye will quickly find the greasy food to help meet its goal.

How can you change this unhealthy belief? Try saying this: "While I'm stressed from work, I can use breath and movement to feel better because I am a conscious, healthy eater." Now, take care to be with these new beliefs and emotions; you are now consciously retraining your brain. If you can turn the subconscious thoughts into conscious actions, over time, your brain will begin to avoid the emotionally driven eating patterns, and instead, turn you toward healthier ways of living your best life. Movin' on with a body filled with good energy and pep will surely be more gratifying.

MOVIN' ON ACTION

The next time you eat an apple, imagine a bright light of pure energy going into your belly. Continue to imagine this light as the apple leaves your stomach, and passes into your organs, muscles, skin, and smile. What does it feel like? How can an apple be so powerful? What if the old adage, "An apple a day keeps the doctor away" was really true? Would you eat an apple? (I hope you would, and make sure it's fresh and straight from the tree)!

_____

_____

_____

_____

_____

_____

THE OPPOSITE OF GOOD ENERGY
IS WEAK OR BAD ENERGY.

Here's a great activity to help you connect to the food you bring into your body: Did you know that the atoms in an apple picked directly from a tree are buzzin' around like crazy, providing the apple with life? The apple is a fresh, vital food. Now, take that same apple and make an apple fritter. First peel it, then mix it in flour, sugar, and fats, and then deep fry it. Cook all the life, all the vitality out of it. Now, take a piece of the apple out of the apple fritter and compare it with a freshly cut piece from the apple off the tree. Think of the word "life." What do you notice? Look closely and imagine what it would look like if you were using a microscope. Does the quality of the apple look different? Can you see the water moving in the freshly cut one, but not the cooked one? What other things do you notice? Does this affect your mind, make it want to eat live, vital foods? (I'm really hoping that it does)!

Remember, when you eat live, vital foods, that live, vital energy is put into your body. That energy is transferred in your body, resulting in beautiful skin and vibrant health.

LET PAIN BE THE OPPORTUNITY TO RETRAIN YOUR BRAIN

So far, this book has been about exploring our inner landscape and finding practical ways to retrain our brains. The underlying theme seems simple, and the approach rather elementary. However, sometimes things just hurt. We can believe that pain is an illusion; we can imagine happy thoughts or we recognize that what we are feeling right now is only temporary. However, we have a physiological body and live in a biological world, and learning how to take the helm through the very real pains that life brings can be difficult.

If we allow pain to be an opportunity for growth, rather than merely a painful feeling to feel, our eyes will be smiling again in no time. If we look at a tree in the early springtime, before the leaves begin to blossom, we see an apparently lifeless tree. If we were to believe that pain is represented by the color brown and happiness by the color green, we could be discouraged. However, with the simple wisdom of knowing that in a few weeks the growth of great, green leaves will bring full life to the tree, we may see joy in the present, and enjoy the brown leaves.

Recognize that in nature, things change, just as they do in our lives. Winter never lasts forever. The person who is present with that pain and can realize that "This too shall pass" has a powerful opportunity to move on.

When in pain, do you look for the green? In other words, can you train your mind and let go of what you don't have and appreciate what you do have? Whatever you are in the midst of, embrace it.

Many years ago, a scientist named Sidney Dancoff proposed a formula that addressed the value of letting pain be an opportunity for growth.

MOVIN' ON ACTION

THE FOUR PAIN EDICTS

If you are in a space that is painful, such as being bullied on social media, I invite you to try this very challenging technique by embodying the following affirmations and questions (Feel free to write down what you experience.)

1. Say to yourself: "While this pain is real, I am not this pain." In other words, if you're being bullied on social media, visualize the hurt you are feeling mystically leaving your body and floating away.

2. "I am supposed to be here, and these emotions I'm feeling are not 'pain' but catalysts designed to energize and guide me to a higher ideal."

3. "Now that I am separated from this pain, what is behind this pain?" For example, could your own self-worth and esteem be reasons why attacks on social media hurt you so much?

4. "Now that I know what is behind the pain, how can I use it to become more than I now am?" How can you improve your self-worth and self-esteem?

Dancoff's formula, known as the "principle of maximum error," states that optimum development occurs when an organism makes the maximum number of mistakes consistent with survival. In other words, the more you screw up, the more you become your best self, provided the screw-up doesn't kill you!

After you are done exploring this technique, go straight into a walking or still meditation. As the meditation progresses, set your intention to really listen and breathe into what you see or hear. If you are ready to let go of the beliefs or imagery that surface, then do so. Pain does not need to exist when you consciously remove the story that is feeding it.

PAIN IS ONLY AS REAL AS THE STORY WE ATTACH TO IT.

Scientists have taken the chemical elements at the root of pain and broken them down into even smaller elements. These elements are involved in certain things other than pain, thus, they are not exclusive to pain. The sub-elements of these chemicals, which present as tiny atoms, can take on the story that pain exudes. Think about when a toddler trips, falls, and begins to cry. If the fall is not that serious, a skilled parent may convince the child that the pain is not real, and in seconds, the child is back up, running around and laughing. If we consciously change our story, we can consciously change our pain.

A while back, I was in the hospital for surgery. Like many, I have a belief that needles cause me great pain. When you think about it, it's just a little poke—and there are, in theory, many things that are more painful than that. I applied the four techniques above, and as the nurse stuck the needle in, all I felt was a mere prick. I could retrain my mind to see it for what it really was: a phobic belief based on some past experience.

Several years ago a friend was sharing how much pain he was in from his recent divorce. I walked him through the four pain edicts, and amazingly, his inner landscape changed instantly. Not only did he realize how much he had to do with the breakup, he fully understood that all the "pain" around him was his own making—that is, his awareness was the control mechanism. Soon, he quit blaming his ex-wife for his pain and began a healing process that has brought him a new level of joy.

When it comes to pain, learn to see it for what it really is: a teacher. Do not let pain have power over you; you are more than the pain. Pain can be such a great teacher. Ask the "teacher" what you are supposed to learn from this experience, a question that leads to a transpersonal wisdom only you can know.

In the end, it's your life. You can design it, shape it, build it, create it, and love it any way you choose.

To put the past behind you, you must accept that you've moved beyond it."

—Ruth from the TV series "Hell on Wheels."

LEARN HOW TO LET PEOPLE MAKE YOU HAPPY.

Living life leads to experiences, and those experiences lead to emotions (some good, some bad, some neither). The tougher experiences may leave scars, and those scars may remind us of our pain, but also that things will get better. German composer Richard Wagner said it so well: "Joy is not in things; it is in us." And while I believe one of the true secrets of happiness is learning how to let people make us happy, the opposite can be true as well. There is no doubt in my mind that we sometimes let people and the negative energy they project affect the very core of our being. It doesn't need to be that way, however, and we can reframe this by saying to ourselves: "Things aren't getting worse: I'm just uncovering them."

I loved Winnie the Pooh growing up. I remember when Winnie would say, "Everybody is alright really." There is truth to that statement, but with one caveat. We don't always live "all right." Don't let the illusion of "all right" keep you from paying your taxes, following up on your responsibilities, or apologizing to those whom you may have wronged. It's safe to say that we need to be aware that everything isn't always alright, but even if it isn't, we can feel all right!

Adopting Winnie's attitude of everything being all right means that we walk down the street differently and that we talk to others and ourselves in a positive way. When we are happy, we vibrate at 1,000 HV/M (happiness vibrations per minute). When we are sad, we vibrate at 100 HV/M. While that number is fictional, there's truth to it. If you are cruising around town at a high vibration, it will be reflected in an upright, confident posture, bright smile, and overall good aura. Just being present with the idea of happiness by smiling (triggering the eighty-something smiling pressure points), surrounding ourselves with happy people, and connecting with them automatically increases our vibrations.

It is easy to lose this vibration awareness. We all know there are so many things distracting us from happiness. The inescapable buzz of the cell phone, Facebook addiction, the news spin cycle, getting the kids to one of their million programs, or squeezing in "you" time—all are things that keep us from just being all right. Stay aware, and don't lose your vibe.

Many researchers believe that our smartphones are making us sad and less aware. Thinking is not necessary when we can Google it, and it is next to impossible to learn something if we can't stay focused enough to allow what we're learning to sink in.

HAVING THE ABILITY TO CONTROL DISTRACTIONS IS THE NEW GENIUS.

I agree with many other scholars that the new "genius" doesn't just have a high IQ or the ability to maintain emotional stability. Rather, the new genius has an innate ability to manage distractions and the discipline to turn off the distractors and to stay aware of who his or her true self is. When our true self is at the forefront, we can vibrate at 1,000 HV/M every day. The person who has the mental state to be able to maintain a high DQ (distraction quotient) can live on track, on purpose, and in a very deliberate way. If we have a high DQ, I really believe we are positioned for success in the future, and everything will always be all right.

Here's a fun test to see if you have a high DQ: Set out an intention to take the stairs instead of the escalator or elevator for the next month (or insert similar challenge here). Next time you are in a public space, such as an airport, and you are texting on your phone or talking to someone and approach an escalator with a stairway right next to it, see what you do. If you take the stairs (something your subconscious lazy brain would not choose), you have high DQ and are mindful. Remember, you are not lazy … your brain is. Don't let your brain run your mind. And continue to be more mindful!

As famed speaker Jim Rohn has said, "There are two types of pain: the pain of discipline and the pain of regret. And while discipline weighs ounces, regret weighs tons." Think of this: Why do some people ride their bikes in the dead of winter in the northern climates? Is it that the bitter cold isn't painful, or is it that the joy of biking to work makes it worth it? Why does one beginner continue to get beaten up by the waves whilst learning to surf, while the other quits after getting pummeled the first time? Why do some people quit school when the going gets tough, while others are capable of earning a doctorate? What are your regrets?

MOVIN' ON ACTION

In the space below, write down a new skill you want to learn. Now think of 2-3 obstacles your brain will create to keep you from committing to learning that skill. What are some creative ways you can mindfully create joy in the process of learning the new skill so you won't subconsciously stop?

_____

_____

_____

_____

_____

_____

_____

We all have challenges that pop up in our lives. There is no question that what happens to you happens to Johnny. And what happens to Johnny happens to Sara—it's called the interconnectedness of life. If you want to do something, like getting that college degree, perhaps, or learning a new skill, and you are not doing it, could it be that you are subconsciously associating that action with pain? What if you were to reframe this association with pain and turn it into the reality of joy? Wouldn't this reality be well worth it?

We need to understand that our minds will always avoid pain and move toward pleasure. The sticky wicket is being mindful enough to know that six hours of watching Netflix is more pleasurable than a five-mile run for most, but in the long run, maybe it's not so healthy. It is also important to recognize that being present in our joy is the secret to success.

FINDING JOY IN THE PROCESS EXCEEDS THE END GOAL.

Even if you've lost your job or you've recently broken up with the love of your life, discovering joy in the process of searching for a new job or meaningful relationship can be yours. My janitor friend was fired from his job and was out of work for nearly two months. Most know him as a positive, happy guy. For him, losing his job meant a new opportunity. He was smart with his money, so he wasn't going to use false "mindfulness" to talk himself into thinking he didn't need to find work eventually. Instead, he had a plan that could carry him a year or so. Further, his belief system told him he was much valued in the janitorial marketplace and could get a job easily.

Even though he believed getting a job would be easy, it didn't look that way from the outset. Similar to the guy who bikes to work in sub-zero weather, he found joy in looking for the job and shaking the hands of potential employers. After two months of really hitting the pavement and pushing out application after application, he found his dream job. Today, he's not just employed, he's the supervisor.

Most folks, after two months of getting rejected, would have become discouraged or bitter, and quit looking. Not my buddy. He stayed positive, spoke in a positive tone, and didn't see not getting a job offer as a "rejection." Whenever you talked to him, he would always be doing all right. Prior to getting hired, each conversation would end with him saying, "If you know of anyone who wants to hire the happiest and hardest-working janitor around, have 'em give me a call." His positive mindset and joy in looking led him to exactly what he wanted.

Faith is like electricity. You can't see it, but you can see the light."

—*Rev. Oswald Chambers*

DIFFERENTIATE THE PAIN THAT HURTS US
FROM THE PAIN THAT CHANGES US.

How can we differentiate the kind of pain that hurts us from the kind that changes us? If we can do this, we have real wisdom. Indeed, some positivists believe that any "unfair" thing that has happened to us can be immediately reframed into a learning experience. While that is philosophically true, the reality is that we are hurting, and all pain changes us. The real wisdom is how we choose to be in a relationship with the beliefs associated with that pain.

If we can learn how first to acknowledge when a belief is debilitating, and then to reframe that belief into one that serves us, that might be our greatest lesson! If we learn to become hyper-aware of this skill, the rest of our lives has the potential to be filled with joy and physical health beyond our wildest imagining.

Several years ago, I brought my aging dog, suffering from several health issues, to the vet. In my heart of hearts, I knew her time was near. I started crying before I could even speak to the vet. The vet was a friend of mine, and he spoke these words, which I will never forget: "Rod, while she may only have a few weeks to live, go be with her, because she may outlive you."

I stopped crying. I looked down, and there she was: still alive, still looking at me. She wouldn't be there forever, but the reality was that she was still there in that moment.

Ishin Yoshimoto, founder of the Naikan Method of Introspection, said it eloquently: "You are fooled by your mind into believing there is tomorrow, so you may waste today."

I took my dog home and she lived for three more happy months.

More than a decade ago, I was training to compete in an ultra-endurance race in Switzerland called the Swiss Gigathlon. It is among the most

You are fooled by your mind into believing there is tomorrow, so you may waste today."

—Ishin Yoshimoto

difficult races in the world. Due to the toughness, the organizers claim that the winner is among the fittest humans in the world. You'll notice I said fittest—not smartest!

To prepare for this grueling race, my dear friend and elite Swiss athlete, Pascal, and I planned on doing a long, four-hour mountain bike training ride across the Swiss Alps to Davos. His girlfriend dropped us off on one side of the mountains and made her way to the other side to pick us up in a few hours. We had plenty of food, and on the mountain, water was abundant. It was a sunny day in June, so we didn't pack a lot of extra clothing. After all, it was a short, straightforward training ride. All we had to do was follow the path over the mountain, eat plenty of food, and manage our energy. Simple.

As we approached the first peak, Pascal, who had already made this ride several times, was perplexed. There was a bit of snow on the ground. "Normally there isn't this much snow on the ground in late June," he said.

We continued to the second peak, where the snow was getting deeper. By the time we got to the top of the third peak, the path had disappeared. Trusting Pascal's Spiderman senses, we playfully continued. We had no fear, and I began to give him some ribbing about getting us lost. He assured me that he knew where we were and where we should go next.

LET CALM BE YOUR GUIDE.

Before we knew it, we were carrying our bikes over our heads through two feet of wet, crusty snow. Our feet were frozen, and we were beginning to show early signs of hypothermia. After five hours of carrying our bikes, we realized we were lost. The humor stopped, and fear began to creep in. We needed to acknowledge we were in a serious situation. We didn't have any extra clothes, our food was limited, and we were in absolute agreement that if we didn't find our way down soon, we would not live through the night.

WHILE DANGER IS VERY REAL, FEAR IS A CHOICE.

We were too far across the Alps to turn back, so we had to act wisely. Our next move would determine our fate. The sun was going down fast, and all we could see was a horizon of mountaintops—there was no sign of Davos. We decided to really think this through, and, using the sun setting in the west as our guide, we broke trail down the snow-packed Alps. After three more treacherous hours of carrying our bikes and our tired bodies through the deep snow, we saw the first sign of light. Davos!

We both yelled in joy, and in the pitch-black night we biked our frozen and totally fatigued bodies into Davos and met Pascal's frightened and worried girlfriend. It was a near-death experience, and we later talked about how the pain of keeping on was far more intense than giving up and hoping help would discover us. We both suspected that deep inside, we would only listen to the voice that said, "Keep on my friend, keep on."

Responding to fear and giving up might have been an unconscious action—but we were totally aware that moving on was our only option. This strength can be yours, too, if you can recognize when you're giving in to the wrong voice in your life instead of moving forward. Make no mistake—while danger is very real, fear is a choice.

I often get asked how the unconscious becomes conscious. First off, the truth is that there is really no such thing as a "conscious mind" or "unconscious mind." There are only varying amounts of conscious-awareness and unconscious-awareness. So, like I said in the Swiss Alps story, the question was: What have I become aware of that I wasn't aware of before?

There was no question that we had to let go of the fact that this wasn't a fictitious situation, and the reality that our lives were in real danger became very clear. In short, we had to get in touch with reality and with the truth in a smart way, but also in a way that could affect our inner compass.

If we are able to expand our consciousness, we will not only be able to see our way down a steep Swiss mountain, but also lift the curtain that is covering up our reality. Perhaps this is enlightenment, perhaps it isn't. In the end, being calm, rather than fearful, brings an expansion of inner knowledge that leads to insight.

The universe was not created to make our lives easy. Life's difficulties

Difficulties are meant to rouse, not discourage. The human spirit is to grow strong by conflict."

—William Ellery Channing

are life's little (or big) educational courses. If a difficult experience such as getting lost in the mountains or developing a cancer teaches us to be more intrinsically aware and more extrinsically communicative, then that's great. The secret is to move beyond the pain of the challenge to the promise of an opportunity. The real tragedy isn't the conflict: it's when we don't let the conflict make our spirit stronger.

It is very easy to fall into the trap of "The world owes me." I know I have felt that way before. Maybe we're dealing with a serious issue at work, and the boss is not recognizing our efforts. One may even say, "I'm angry right now, and I feel disrespected. I am going to call my boss and tell her she's lucky to have me working for her, as I could be working somewhere better."

Be careful not to react to this inner voice. Instead, let these thoughts play out while doing a meditation or exercise session rather than when you're at work. These feelings you have are real, and perhaps a good heart-to-heart needs to take place to sort out what's on your mind. The key is first to become aware that you are angry, and that anger carries with it a certain body language, tone of voice, and select set of words. It should come as no surprise that approaching the situation from the lens of anger will most likely be poorly received (and may even put you out of a job). While in your meditation, think about how you can use the energy anger gives you to create an opportunity. Once you do this, you will reverse your body language, tone of voice, and words. Now, stay with this awareness when you meet your boss. Use your communication skills and personal experience to reframe your concerns with an energy that is direct, yet compassionate and non-aggressive. You might reframe it as something like: "I'm not going to tell her off. I'm going to calm down, be respectful, stay with my breath, and say (xyz)."

── MOVIN' ON ACTION ──

Write down the name of someone who is getting under your skin. Now mindfully navigate your inner voice from one of anger to one of compassion. Sit with this for a few minutes. What thoughts and words come to mind?

_____

_____

_____

_____

_____

_____

_____

_____

_____

BEING CALM INSTEAD OF ANGRY LEADS TO INSIGHT.

As you practice this approach in your mind, you may find a general sense of relief rolling through your body, beginning at your head and ending at your toes. If you can stay alert and speak from the lens of compassion, you are ready to address the boss or fellow co-worker about the charged issue.

If you really think about it, we are just floating around in life, and our time is limited. While the spirit may carry on, now is the time. Your boat is floating.

Life is like stepping onto a boat that is about to sail out to sea and sink."

—Shunryu Suzuki, Sōtō Zen monk

I often think of the millions of humans who get into their cars and commute to work ... work a long day ... get back in the car and drive back home ... turn on the TV, tune out, eat, go to bed ... and repeat. This is fun? Your boat is sinking! Now is the time to forgo "making a living" and instead, design your life! Again, it's a belief. You can still get in your car and "go to work," but with an attitude of gratitude.

I am discouraged when I see hard work and perseverance being thought of as negative. It's important to rejoice in your accomplishments. You earned that feeling! We all know that Jesus Christ said, "Do unto others as you would have them do unto you" (Matthew 7:12). Might you reverse that, and say, "Don't do unto yourself what you would not do unto others"? If you would not shoot down your friend's big dream or tell him to give up when the going gets tough, then don't do it to yourself either. In other words, be very careful what you think and say about yourself, because you may attract that belief, and it will become your reality. Again, all the universal experiences were designed for you!

CAN WE SHIFT FROM FEAR TO TRUST?

I have a lot of great friends. Some are very successful, and some struggle to get by. When I really think about the difference between those who succeed at finding contentment as opposed to those who struggle, I notice one thing. The ones who succeed have an underlying authentic belief that things will just work out. This magical way of thinking may seem trite or overly simplified, but it is true. What is funny is that the opposite is true, too. If we think things won't go our way and will never work out, that will come to pass, as well. My really good friend, Al, knows that things will go his way. He has an uncanny belief pattern that starts with the finish line. He wanted a new house, so he learned how to build a house and built his own. He wanted to be in a band, so he took up the bass guitar, formed a band, and was rockin' in front of the masses. He wanted to be a doctor, and now he's a physician's assistant doing what he loves to do. He wanted to be in a loving relationship, and now he's married and has great kids.

Things may not be as we plan them, but if we believe we will be okay on the inside, we will always be okay, no matter the external circumstances.

Musician and life coach John Tesh embraces these five cardinal rules for life:

1. Make peace with your past, so it won't disturb your present.

2. What other people think of you is none of your business.

3. Time heals almost everything—give it time.

4. No one oversees your happiness. Only you can cultivate it.

5. Don't compare your life to others, and don't judge them. You have no idea what their journey is all about.

While positive thinking can't get you everything, it can get you anything better than negative thinking will."

—*Zig Ziglar*

POSITIVE SELF-TALK IS ATTRACTIVE.

A family member of mine has been struggling with her living situation lately. Last winter she was asked to move out of her house because her landlord sold it. Her comment to me was something along the lines of, "These types of things always happen to me, so of course he would sell the house in the middle of winter and kick me and my child out!"

She was hurting, and we had a small conversation about how her beliefs shape the person she is right now—the person who happens to be having struggles with her living situation. We decided that if she wanted to find a solution, first she needed to find a way to change her beliefs and attitudes surrounding this situation.

We went on to play with ideas and try to create a new set of beliefs. This is not hocus-pocus; it can be fun and uplifting. She started with this new self-talk: "This opportunity will allow me to find a place that suits my space and financial situation better." She felt herself resonate with this statement and began to repeat it. After just a week and a few phone calls, she was talking to friends in a more positive tone of voice.

Then, her next-door neighbor offered her his house, which turned out to be much better. In short, in addition to finding a new place to live, she became much more content than she had been the previous week by simply changing her self-talk.

We all can do this, and even if we don't get the house, positive self-talk, or having faith, is more attractive, more desirable, and more rewarding than self-pity or a negative demeanor.

Kris Henry is a senior process expert at a local hospital in Minnesota and leads teams in the Lean Six Sigma Process Improvement Methodology. I asked Kris to answer some questions. After reading them, maybe you can write your answers on a separate piece of paper.

WHAT LIES IN THE SPACE BETWEEN COURAGE AND CONFIDENCE?

Fear. Confidence is what happens when you know what to do, aren't worried about the results, and perhaps have some expertise in the area. Courage may look the same as confidence, but the difference is that to be courageous you must over-come some sort of fear. Fear of the unknown or maybe fear of the result of your actions. I had a fridge magnet for years that read, "Leadership is the ability to hide your panic." Related to my work life, it's been my mantra, and it's part of how I moved from courage to confidence. One could probably substitute courage for leadership... "Courage is the ability to hide your panic." My puppy pulled the magnet off the side of the fridge a couple weeks ago and chewed it up. Considering that I've been thinking of starting up something on my own and have yet to work up the courage to act—I wonder if it was a sign.

HOW CAN ONE CONTROL THAT CRAZY INNER VOICE THAT EITHER DRAWS YOU TOWARD, OR KEEPS YOU AWAY, FROM LIVING YOUR BEST LIFE?

About ten years ago I read a story about a monk who held the belief that other people's opinions and actions should not influence our choices. "If you give your best effort and always do what is right morally, other opinions should not mat-ter," he claimed. It's an extremely liberating philosophy, because I no longer make choices based on what I think other people want me to do, but I always try to do the right thing. What the right thing to do may not always be completely clear; there-fore, I've had to learn to always trust my "gut" and do the best I can. If it doesn't seem right, it's probably not. It's true that where you are right now and what you are doing is directly related to decisions you make. I really try to own my decisions, whether they turn out to be correct or not.

WHAT IS THE DIFFERENCE BETWEEN CHRISTIAN PRAYER AND MEDITATION?

That's an easy one for me because of my strong belief in the afterlife and God. Christian prayer is talking to God ... meditation is being quiet and still, so He can talk back.

WHAT DOES IT FEEL LIKE TO SAY, "I FAILED" INSTEAD OF "I JUST GOT A RESULT THAT I DON'T WANT"?

Self-esteem and self-worth play a large role in these two outcomes. If your self-worth comes from the effort, doing your best, and knowing you did what you could, then the latter should be the outcome. If your self-worth is tied up in what other people will think, that they will think you failed, then the former is probably the outcome.

WHAT'S THE DIFFERENCE BETWEEN PROCRASTINATION AND BEING TOO LAZY? AND WHY?

Procrastination can occur when one is afraid of the outcome or anticipates an effort that won't be enjoyable. Laziness is not caring.

WHAT IS THE DIFFERENCE BETWEEN FEAR AND LACK OF KNOWING?

I don't think these are different. Lack of knowing can cause fear, but fear can probably also be caused by something you know will happen. For instance, if you had a painful medical procedure and must have it performed again, you might be afraid of the pain you know will occur. Mostly, however, fear and lack of knowing are closely related. People live their whole lives not doing things because they are afraid of what might happen. For this, I take a lesson from the Navy Seals. Seal training is one of the hardest things imaginable. Some recruits choose to quit in anticipation of not being able to do the training for that day, so they could quit at any time without shame. I would choose to at least try.

HOW CAN YOU CHANGE YOUR MINDSET FROM FEAR TO PLAYFULNESS?

Aside from gaining knowledge and experience to reduce fear, the best way I've found to change my mindset is to "pretend" or make it my reality through mindful practice. I use visualization to trick my mind into not being fearful. Once the fear in my mind is neutralized, I can consciously manifest a positive outcome.

ARE THERE VARIOUS MIND STATES?

Yes, and I believe each mind state represents the evolution of life. Since I believe in reincarnation, I think this evolution is related to how "old" your soul is. Young souls are unaware, going through life on autopilot, making mistakes and not learning from them. Older souls are aware of their actions and learn from mistakes. They may even start to be self-aware but are self-centered in this regard. Self-centeredness can materialize as either low self-esteem or arrogance. The next evolution is also self-awareness, but also awareness of your impact on others, and the world around you. I believe there's another mind state, which is full awareness of the world around you without regard to self. Examples include people like Mother Teresa or Gandhi, who dedicated their lives to the service of others, and no longer have any need for material things or personal comforts.

HOW CAN ONE REFRAME INNER THOUGHTS?

I've always wondered why sometimes we readily admit mistakes and sometimes never do, even when the proof we are wrong is overwhelming. Maybe it relates to how much of our self-worth is tied up in what other people think. The more of your self-worth that comes from within, the less it matters if you were wrong about something. I've also read some things about testing or experimentation in life recently. People who are always testing in life are probably more able to admit that something didn't work because they are always looking for ways to improve.

GROWTH IS OPTIONAL, CHANGE IS NOT

BEING MINDFULLY ACTIVE IN YOUR OWN PSYCHOLOGY

It has been said that life is change, but growth is optional. Over the years, I've had a wonderful life filled with achievement in endurance sports, successful businesses, two great sons, and some very positive relationships as well as some challenging ones. I've had accidents, like the one where I was hit by a car in a bike race, which resulted in a broken wrist and vertebrae. After my divorce, I had some unhealthy fights over custody, and I've had my share of disagreements with my business partners. Whether good or bad, these experiences weren't enough to change my personality. I have been graced with my fair share of positive media stories surrounding my achievements and businesses and have also endured a few stories that weren't positive. Public figures are often subjects of gossip, and I am no exception!

You may have heard the old saying: "God made food for the birds but did not put it in the nest." It is no secret that we need to act to find our happiness, as it will not simply arrive. The "bluebird of happiness" really is just a myth! Being mindfully active in our own psychology and mental health is the secret to finding growth in life's inevitable changes.

Have you ever looked up only to see the world dumping everything on you? At any age or time in our lives, we may feel like life isn't treating us fairly. Have you ever felt like you had been treated unfairly? It can be an overwhelming experience. Questions swirl in all directions: "How can my life spin onto a totally different path in a blink of an eye?" "Is it

God's will?" "Is it destiny?" "What lessons am I to take from this?" "Is this random?" "Am I a bad person?" "Am I a good person who's been treated badly?" "Am I a victim?" "Am I somewhat to blame, but not totally?" "How in the hell can I make this swirling energy stop?"

What I've learned through my life experiences has been nothing short of amazing. I have reflected on my own life and relationships and how I have responded to my friends. I've considered my intimate relationships, my business relationships, and my relationship with the universe, as well. What I've learned is that in seeking growth, one can forge a good and happy life.

I learned from Jim Rohn that in questioning our daily life activities, we can ask the foolish, selfish question, "What am I getting from this experience?" Or we can be wise about it, and ask, "Who am I becoming from this experience?" And, if we are becoming a person who develops greater awareness, is more authentic in relationships, and lives life to a higher ideal, then we will grow, and we will be more successful and content.

Making sense of this mystical thing called life is a journey in and of itself. As I stated earlier, there are two types of pain. There's the pain of discipline, and there's the pain of regret. Living a life without regret requires discipline. We all know it's hard to apply discipline to our lives, but sooner or later, understanding that the pain of regret usually weighs heavier than the pain of discipline is a healthy awareness. The key is to be awake enough to realize when we are confusing the two.

TRAIN THE UNCONSCIOUS—ARE YOU A KNOWER?

Abraham Maslow reminds us that many believe we live in a dualistic world. There's the knower and the known, us and them, body and brain. The point where you can fully experience life is when the two become one. Maslow states that when we go from observing something to making it part of us, we escape dualism and achieve oneness or monistic thinking. The box-office hit *Avatar* is a great example of the monistic way of thinking. The blue creatures in the movie (the Na'vi) are one with nature, with all other sentient beings. When they kill something for food, they believe energy from the kill goes into their bodies, and the circle of life continues—oneness. Achieving monistic thinking is enlightenment. But it requires a shift in your way of thinking. To do this, we must get out of our heads and into our hearts and bellies.

MOVIN' ON ACTION

To begin training yourself to think monistically like the Na'vi, set your intention to drop your energy from your head down to your gut. You can do this using the Mindful Attention Posture (MAP) developed by Dr. Glenn Hartelius to help people manage stress and be more efficient with their energy. Here's how:

Sit comfortably in your chair. Take your pointer finger and press it between your eyebrows (the third eye). Take your finger away. Now imagine the place where your finger was being a portal to your brain. Open the portal and see an energy ball the size of a marble as it enters your head. Allow this energy ball to hover in the middle of your brain. Feel its heat and allow the energy ball to slide down the front of your cervical spine and stop in your throat. If you feel a choking sensation, mindfully release it. After a few seconds, see the energy ball follow the front of the spine and drop down to your heart. Feel the heat, and sense how this energy can think and feel as though it were your brain. Some "heartfelt" thoughts may arise at this point. Acknowledge them and gently let them go. Now allow the energy ball to follow the front of your spine down into the gut, about two inches below your belly button. This is your energy center—your core. Again, just be aware, and feel this energy in your core region. What do you sense? If you find yourself going "back up into your head," mindfully bring the energy ball back down to your core.

Allow your five senses to radiate from this area. Feel the air on your skin from your core. Smell the various scents from your core, and so on. Stay with this awareness for a few minutes, and then allow the ball of energy to grow. There are no real edges to this energy. See it growing and growing, eventually encompassing the whole body, and at least three feet around it. Allow this energy, with your core being the nucleus, to bring you a higher sense of calm. Allow your heart rate to come down and calm your spirit. As you continue to practice the MAP, it will become automatic and will increase your ability to respond more mindfully to all of life's offerings. Practice this powerful technique when you exercise, give a presentation, or deal with a stressful event. Soon it will become your default, and you'll think and act more deliberately and compassionately.

WHAT DO WE SEE? SEEING WITH
OUR UNCONSCIOUS EYE.

Have you ever noticed that when you buy a red car, you suddenly identify with other, similar cars on the road? You may even find yourself giddily waving at the driver of another red car, as if you share something deeply in common. Did everyone else buy a red car the same day you did? Or maybe you are walking in the mall, when amongst the thousands of people, you happen to spot someone else with a Detroit Tigers hat. As a Detroit fan, you feel compelled to go up and high-five a stranger. My friend, Jason, an avid Tigers fan, does this all the time. These are simple examples of the reticular activating system (RAS), a system in which your unconscious eye sifts through the myriad of visual stimuli in the environment to pick out what is important to your conscious eye.

If we learn the steps we must take to benefit properly from the RAS system, our eyes will find whatever it is that can move us toward our goals, inspirations, and aspirations. This speaks to the old-fashioned technique of writing down our goals. When we write something down and meditate on it with a bit of emotion, we make what wasn't important matter. Speaking to others about our goal anchors the importance of our intention, as well.

We cannot turn off the RAS. We are going to look for what is important, whether we like it or not. The key is to make important what we want to be important rather than what the world wants us to believe is important.

If you are looking for a good job, examine yourself to see whether you're willing to work hard and sacrifice, or if you're just looking for Easy Street. If you are willing to truly throw yourself into your work and improve yourself, make it important by meditating on the intention, writing down a goal, speaking of it to others, etc. Like seeing that Detroit Tigers hat, the unconscious will tell your eyes to go to work looking for that thing. This will lead you to success by subconsciously bringing resources and knowledge to you.

David Brooks, in his book *The Social Animal*, says that the average human being has thousands of unconscious thoughts every minute. In the same minute, however, that same human is capable of only a few conscious thoughts. Movin' on is about training the unconscious to help

MOVIN' ON ACTION

Reticular activating system (RAS) is a system in which your unconscious eye sifts through the myriad of visual stimuli in the environment to pick out what is important to your conscious eye. Here is how to set an intention to activate RAS:

Think about something you would like to occur and write down this goal using very clear language. Then meditate on it, pray about it, and/or speak of it to others to anchor its importance in your life. Write down some things you can associate this goal with to increase the emotional intensity. Again, if it is really important to you, your subconscious mind will find solutions.

_____

_____

_____

_____

_____

the conscious move you toward what you want out of life. So, if you are looking to improve your health, make that important. Set your intention to find a trainer to help you achieve your goal. Once you've done this, you may notice a flier at your workplace that reads, "Personal Training— First session free." What's interesting is that flier may have been on that wall for over two months. You probably walked by it forty times. Again, what is important to the mind, the eyes will see.

It is not healthy to be thinking all the time. Thinking is intended for acquiring knowledge or applying it. It is not essential for living."

—Yogi and Sanskrit scholar Ernest Wood

Just a gentle reminder that this is not a thinking technique: it's a mindfulness technique. Move what is important out of your head and into your gut and energy body. Using the mindful attention posture (MAP) we learned previously, move the energy and thoughts from your monkey brain (first brain) down into your gut (second brain).

Even Freud recognized that he needed to analyze himself before psychoanalyzing his patients. Finding the energy to analyze oneself can be difficult. Some people ruminate and spin over a situation, trying to make sense of it. While this can be paralyzing, if used wisely, ruminating can bring about solutions.

Keep a pen and pad close by, and whenever your ruminating brain comes up with a thought, write it down. This is not to say that you will act on the thought, but it puts it out there, so you can embody what, where, and how you want to handle the situation.

Examining a thought that came to you for no apparent reason usually has some merit. How you act on that thought, preferably in a wise and authentic way, frames how your day will look.

Using the aforementioned techniques, you can be as Freud, analyzing and embodying the solutions to the obstacles and problems that crop up in your everyday life.

MOVIN' ON ACTION

If you are having a hard time getting into your core, here's another approach, the Quick Coherence Technique (QCT). This technique, much like the **MAP** mentioned earlier, was developed by the Institute of HeartMath. There are three simple steps to the QCT technique:

1. Imagine your thoughts are taking an elevator down from your brain to your heart.
2. Now, begin to breathe a bit deeper and into your heart. Imagine the air going in and then out of the heart.
3. Think of some positive thoughts. You can think of a time when something fun or positive happened to you or something you are thankful for. Stay with this for a few minutes and then jot down how it felt. The act of writing it down will increase its importance and will anchor that feeling.

_____

_____

_____

_____

_____

_____

_____

10

THE STATE OF BEING
KIND, HUMBLE, AND AWARE

KINDNESS AND VULNERABILITY ARE NOT WEAKNESSES.

K indness is often mistaken for weakness, but it is not about letting people walk all over us. Kindness is a quality that resonates at such a high level, has so many layers, and allows us to rise above our feelings of weakness. Staying present with compassion leads us to kind actions, which is never, ever a mistake. But it begins with compassion. So, if we are struggling with solutions on how to handle a problem, we may be one-hundred-percent assured that by approaching the situation with kind intentions, we will lay the foundation for positive conscious actions later on. According to Thich Nhat Hanh, "It is like growing lotus flowers. Without suffering, we have no way to learn to understand with compassion."

HUMILITY—THE FOUNDATION TO MOVIN' ON.

I believe that Jesus's main message was one of humility. Nearly all accounts of his life reflect this. However, let's not confuse humility with low self-esteem. I struggle with some Christian churches that seem to take the verse "God resists the proud but gives grace to the humble" to the next level. I have witnessed churches having parishioners share all the ways they have "sinned and have fallen short of the glory of God." While being humble and recognizing we will fall short is a healthy way to look at our lives, to my mind, repeatedly admonishing oneself only creates more neural-pathways that do not enhance our lives. There's but a thin line between being so self-deprecating that we damage our self-esteem and sense of self and being so adamantly proud that we can't admit our shortcomings.

Have you ever felt terrible about a situation you weren't responsible for? Or felt a little overconfident at a time when you probably should have been more humble, I know I have. From my perspective, the solution is getting out of "self," realizing there is a bigger world out there beyond my own and reminding myself I'm not the center of the universe. In short, most of us may benefit from a dose of humility, but all of us need a dose of self-love in those areas of life in which we tend to beat ourselves up. A good lesson is from a song in the musical *Oklahoma!:* "I ain't sayin' that I'm better than anybody else, but I'll be damned if I ain't just as good!"

KEEP OUR COMPETENCE ABOVE OUR CONFIDENCE.

We all have blind spots. There are blind spots in how we view ourselves, how we view others, and how we see compassion, wisdom, and life itself. When we are looking to make positive change, we can seek the advice of others who may help us see where we're blinded or stuck in ego. For many, this is an ongoing challenge. I know it is for me, and I've often wondered what the difference is, exactly, between being confident and being cocky? My good friend, Dr. Chris Delp, says, "If your confidence is greater than your competence, others may see you as cocky." Keep your competence above your confidence.

Being able to humbly think and reflect on who you are is a fun but difficult practice. Henry Ford once said, "Thinking is the hardest work there is, which is probably the reason why so few engage in it."

I have a few affirmations that I use. If someone says I am bad, or not good at something, and I believe differently, I will say to them (or just to myself): "I am sorry you feel that way; I know differently." If I am accused of something that I don't believe is my issue or that I am guilty of, I will ask myself: "Is this so?" The key is to immediately reframe the statement to change the negative implication and thus, neutralize the painful negative potential.

MOVIN' ON ACTION

Write down a moment in your life when a random assumption popped into your head. For example, one day when you were at work and a colleague looked at you with a furrowed brow, did you take that look personally or did you make a negative assumption about the look?

Now do the **MAP** and be with that experience. Were you able to depersonalize and neutralize the assumption? After all, do you truly know what this person was thinking?

If you believe that they can't "read your mind," then you need to believe that you cannot read theirs.

_____

_____

_____

_____

_____

_____

_____

_____

PURPOSEFULLY SURROUND YOURSELF
WITH POSITIVE PEOPLE.

Healthy people like to be surrounded by happy, positively energetic, confident, content people. This can be you, if you are able to be alert enough to present your best self to the world. I can't stress strongly enough that this is a belief. Armed with your new beliefs, you may be prompted to buy your friends a gift, cook a meal, or manifest the good in everything. Believe in the power of your awesomeness, while recognizing and actively working to correct your shortcomings.

The most important takeaway, here, is always to align yourself with your new belief or new story. While aligned with your new belief, feel with your heart what it feels like—as if it has already been done, even if it hasn't. Put yourself in that place in the future right now. Can you feel the resulting joy, the expression of appreciation? This is how we manifest what we desire, and it helps to anchor the new belief.

Believing in the mystery of all this can be difficult. It will be infinitely harder, however—if not impossible—to make it happen if you don't believe in it. I have a degree in teaching Life Science, so I used to believe that I needed either rigorous scientific proof or a concrete example in order to believe in something.

I'm asking you to believe in the power of accepting ambiguity. The neural cells that are found in your brain are also in your heart. You are capable of your greatest good when the heart and the mind are in alignment. This synergy has energy and an ability that no one can explain. Worst-case scenario: In the process of striving for this alignment, you will become a more positive person. Why not the advice of Nike® and "Just Do It"?

BEING AT PEACE WITH AMBIGUITY IS ENLIGHTENMENT.

I am not saying we should believe in all of this naïvely. Being naïve will only bring us more confusion. Being at peace with ambiguity is modern-day enlightenment. Our inner landscape and awareness will lead us to a new set of tools and realities that will wake us up and direct us on a path to optimal living. This is a path filled with good friends, happy relationships, and overall well-being. Changing our beliefs is that easy. Being humble enough to change our beliefs, and/or believing we can change them, are the difficult parts.

Eleanor Roosevelt said, "You gain strength, courage, and confidence by every experience in which you really stop to look fear in the face…. You must do the thing you think you cannot do."

There is no doubt that I have had some awesome relationships, and I have had some painful ones. Being alert enough to fully experience both is what makes life so juicy. We experience many feelings: anger, elation, depression, fulfillment, hatred, freedom, disgust, and happiness. We can use all of them as fuel to frame our new beliefs toward relationships.

GETTIN' FROM THE DAY.

A friend of mine has been teaching communications at a respected college. He's been there for years, but he'd much rather be at home doing his art. He treads his way through the day, watching the clock and doing the minimum. While he may wish to quit his job, the truth is, he needs the money to support his family. How could he change his mindset from one that gets through the day in a painful, "I hate this crap" kind of a way to one that embraces the positives and gets what it can from the day?

A colleague from El Salvador sometimes talks about street children who are so poor they rummage through garbage piles to find what they can for the day. It's tragic, but they're doing what they must do to survive. We have all heard it: One person's trash is another's treasure.

If those street children can handle their situation, we can learn to adapt to our situation, too. We may find it painful, demeaning, or less than our skill set warrants. Perhaps we will make a change, but while we are in that position, we can set the intention to find the "treasure in the day." Even if your job is the lowliest, dirtiest job ever, say, cleaning toilets, you can set the intention to be the happiest, best damn toilet cleaner there is! It's okay to have some fun along the way.

Author Ernestine Ulmer said, "Life is uncertain. Eat dessert first." Sometimes we don't need to delay gratification, and sometimes we can let discipline just fall to the side. Life is meant to be lived, not endured.

Oedipus was a smart guy. He realized that as we grow through life, we go through stages. A baby crawling on all fours is totally dependent. He finds his first pivotal turning point when he can "stand on his own two feet." At this point, he is walking through life, making friends, earning a

What is the creature that walks on four legs in the morning, two legs at noon, and three in the evening?"

—Riddle of the Sphinx

"Man."

—Oedipus, answering the riddle

living, meeting his mate, and building his future. Then, as life goes on, and he ages, he eventually gets to his second turning point. He needs a cane, or third foot. This cane speaks of the aging body and all that goes with that. But the real question is this: Are we growing up, or just growing old?

YOU ARE OLDER NOW THAN YOU WERE WHEN YOU STARTED READING THIS.

One of my doctor friends shared with me the fact that your bones are constantly regenerating. Your bones are very much alive and malleable. He added that he could discern someone's happiness by the bone structure between their eyes. He said, "If someone is constantly frowning and furrowing their brow, their forehead will eventually develop a bone extrusion to facilitate the muscles needed to support that constant frown." The same holds true for the bones supporting your smiling muscles. Does your face have a smiling bone structure or one that frowns? If you have a frowning face, take some advice from my seventy-year-old mentor, Dr. Gene Ley.

Gene was in my triathlon camp for twenty years, the chair of my master's degree committee, and one of the happiest guys I've ever met. I remarked when I first met him that he had such beautiful, smiling eyes. You would see him walking down the hallway at the university pushing his cart to lecture, and he would have this huge grin. I would ask, "What are ya smiling about, Gene?" He would respond, "Am I smiling?" We would laugh, and he would continue to class. He stayed active in my triathlon camp well into his seventies and even though he died recently, I'm sure he is still smiling.

With age, one can see changes in a person such as deepened insight, a renewed way of letting go of old habits, and outgrowing old ways of thinking. Getting old can be hard, but it can also be the best time of your life. It all depends on how we've been projecting our energy from the inside out. The lines on our faces tell the story, and positive energy is reflected by crow's feet around our eyes that wrinkle upward. We want "smiling eyes"!

The Tibetans believe that living for positive energy is not only the best way to live your life, it is the best way to leave it, too. In the world of quantum mechanics research, many believe that the energy you project is transferred in and around the universe. We all know the universe is not here to make our lives better, but we have the power to make the universe and those around us better.

It is important to note that what we think, we will eventually say; and what we say, we will eventually do; and what we do repeatedly will sooner or later shape our character. In summary, our character, or the way the world sees us, is the result of our inner voice. Mindfully choosing the right words leads to smiling eyes!

MOVIN' ON: STAND AND DELIVER

KEVIN PRECKEL: One of Minnesota's top educators, Kevin Preckel worked at a Minnesota juvenile detention center, where he taught some of the toughest kids around. For years he felt out of place, until he discovered

a simple yet profound way to connect with the students. He shares his story below:

I've worked at a northern Minnesota juvenile center for thirteen years. I never applied for the job. I was on a temporary license, and I was placed here. I needed a job, but I really didn't like it.

We have no idea who we're going to get for students, because it's whoever gets arrested. It was very hard to plan. A lot of the skills you learn just don't apply here. I might have taught grades 7 to 12, but ability-wise they range from grades 3 to 12. We will even sometimes get students who have already graduated.

If there were difficulties with behaviors. There are two adults in the room supervising behaviors, each with different approaches, different expectations, different rules, etc. And there I was in my second year, a newer teacher trying to figure things out.

After a while, a couple kids would ask for a book, and I'd give it to them. I could start to see a budding connection there. They'd ask for a book, and I'd bring it from home and say, "You can borrow it to read." Subsequently, I started asking the school for more money for the library, and they delivered.

Today there's a substantial library for kids looking to recalculate their way in life. The number of kids who are reading is really gratifying. It may seem overly simple or trite, but I use books to connect to the students. It's generated some very interesting conversations and questions. For me, I found a simple yet meaningful way to turn a hard situation into something where I was able to connect with the students and ultimately, myself.

Kevin felt like trying to reach his students was hopeless. Movin' on meant using this as a springboard for an effective opportunity. The joy on a student's face from something as simple as a book was powerful, and the connections he built there helped guide young offenders to a better future.

The great psychologist, Carl Jung, wrote, "There is no coming to consciousness without pain." If it weren't for the difficult times in life, we'd never really know life's beauty. For these kids, how long do they have to live with their pain? Answer: until they become conscious of their behavior. Perhaps something as simple as a book can wake them up?

Robert Schuller was right when he said, "Tough times never last; tough people do." And no matter what we've gone through, there is hope. By now we know we have the power to change the way our mind speaks, and we can find relevance in most everything we do. Are you willing to stay with your practice for as long as it takes?

11

DO WE HAVE THE FORTITUDE AND WISDOM TO THINK CRITICALLY?

The world is a dangerous place, not because of those who do evil, but because of those who look on and do nothing.
—Albert Einstein

NAVIGATING GROUPTHINK WISELY.

Being able to think critically and to share those thoughts eloquently are two key traits of wise people and are essential to movin' on. Lemmings follow the other lemmings both physically and intellectually. It's natural to want to be part of a group. But groupthink can be scary, especially when the crowd starts going in a direction that doesn't line up with your beliefs or morals. When the whole group thinks one way, it's like a large freighter entering the harbor. If it is off course, the captain can't simply make a sharp turn or stop the boat. It's going to take a mile for that thing to turn or to stop. Like the large group, it's hard to stop. So be careful about getting on the boat with a captain who doesn't look or think ahead.

This can also be positive, for example, like on a playground when one child decides to organize a game, and everyone decides to join in, and fun ensues. However, on that same playground on the very next day a kid decides to tease someone, and everyone joins in.

Groupthink can happen with our family and/or with close friends. For example, there might be some jealousy or envy if you were to receive a new job or decided to embark on a healthier lifestyle. To find balance in their jealous and envious minds, people may try to convince others to work against you. If you're trying to lose weight, maybe they tell others you're getting too skinny, or say you're overdoing it. Winning others over to their jealous beliefs and applying unnecessary pressure on you makes them feel better about their own inability to change. You must mindfully stick to your goal and be aware that jealousy, envy, or other wasted emotions are really a deflection—they want what you have. The solution is not to defend yourself, but rather to send them a compassionate thought or thank them for giving you the juice to keep movin' on. I liken this to one of my favorite quotes, by author Michael Larsen: "A diamond is a piece of coal that stuck to the job."

If we choose to hang around people who spill compassion, we are filled with substance and embrace culture; we will become like them. Avoid becoming a lemming that follows activities that don't align with your values. Be critically mindful with whom you hang out and what you absorb. It's too easy to follow the masses. A conscious choice to hang around people and family members who bring you happiness is a choice to move toward becoming your best self.

GO WHERE THE EXPECTATIONS ARE
HIGH AND THE LAUGHTER IS LOUD.

My dad used to say, "If you hang around with dirty dogs, you're going to get fleas." Quite often, when someone has been hurt, they avoid people altogether or connect with others who support their low-vibrating mindset (depression). Being conscious of which crowd one associates with is a powerful awareness exercise. I tell those I coach to make a conscious effort to go where the expectations are high and the laughter is loud.

If you currently have a low-vibrating energy, it's important to be aware so as not to be fooled by your brain's desire to seek like-minded people or activities (i.e., low-energy people, mindless TV, mind-altering substances, or no one at all). Remember, your brain works for your mind and heart. Teach it to behave the way you want it to behave.

Psychologist and author Rollo May remarked, "The opposite of courage in our society is not cowardice, it's conformity." For example, when it comes to critical thinking about a situation, forming an opinion and standing up for our beliefs is difficult and takes courage. To just sit back and let someone hurt us or hurt someone else is cowardice.

We see this on the Internet also with troll culture, whether it's celebrity rumors or personal bullying. When a cowardly blogger anonymously posts negative and unfounded comments and others follow, this is groupthink. This viral feed gathers impetus much like a snowball rolling down a mountain, pulling others along, resulting in an avalanche of hurtful commentary. You do not want to conform to this, right? Beyond that avalanche, no one knows how the human being on the other end is feeling.

Make no bones about it, quantum physics shows us that the faceless blogger, filled with negative thoughts, will probably suffer more. It would be an interesting study to see how happy, spiritually balanced, and socially connected those who regularly blog hateful and hurtful comments really are. My suspicion is that happiness is higher for those who generally look for the good in all people and know spiritual health.

I want to be clear that there is a large distinction between stating facts to illuminate people on a subject you are all discussing, versus negatively writing things that are intended to hurt. Standing up for what's right is always good, but check your motivations first, so as not to manifest false information into the groupthink universe.

GETTING TOXICITY OUT OF OUR LIVES IS A DECISION.

It should come as no surprise that we all have toxic people in our lives. Sometimes, no matter how positive we are, people will try to tear us down. They may lie about us or do things to hurt us. Preacher Charles Haddon Spurgeon said, "A lie can travel halfway around the world while the truth is putting on its shoes." The good news is, the truth will eventually get even. If you are Galileo, it may take a while, but it will get there! It is a useless waste of energy to try to change the person who is tearing you down. We cannot change other people; we can only change ourselves.

We need to be disciplined enough to resist engaging in angry "facebook-ing" or other social media posts; doing so will only hurt us. We all know how hard it is to be humble, and that is why so few are. Don't underestimate the power of humility followed by a good face-to-face conversation to clear the air. It is good medicine.

Sometimes, no matter how much we wish to communicate or get something off our chests, it's just not going to happen. While you can't force someone to talk to you, you can rearrange your mindset to better adapt to another's. I used to think that my old girlfriend shouldn't smoke. I would push this non-smoking agenda on her all the time and let her know all the facts about smoking. She would listen, light up, and keep on smoking. In other words, she didn't have a problem with smoking—I did. As time went on, my reaction became more charged, and long after we had broken up, she eventually did quit. For all I know, my pushiness was the reason she kept smoking for as long as she did!

We have a choice in how we respond to others. I was in a seminar where the speaker said he used to be so naïve as to think that liars shouldn't lie, or cheaters shouldn't cheat. He went on playfully to say that they're called liars and cheaters for a reason—it's in their job description, their nature.

You may have heard the story of the scorpion and the frog: It came to pass that deep in the woods, a scorpion approached a frog.

"Friend," the scorpion said, "you know I cannot swim, but I must pass over the river. Will you let me ride on your back across?"

"Oh, scorpion," the frog said. "You know I love to help all the creatures of the forest, and I give rides to the small ones who can't swim whenever they ask. But I have heard of you—that you sting all who would help you."

"Friend frog," the scorpion said. "I would not sting you, for I cannot swim. If I were to sting you, you would sink, and I would drown."

This made sense to the frog, so he allowed the scorpion to climb upon his back, and they began to cross the river. But when he was halfway across, the frog felt a sharp sting on his back.

"But scorpion," he cried out as he began to sink, "why would you sting me? Now we shall both perish."

"I can't help it," the scorpion responded. "It's in my nature."

Some people are just scorpions. Unlike in the parable above, they can change, but only if they truly want to.

I had a running acquaintance who was a stockbroker. I didn't know him well. He told me he wanted to give me a chance to get in on a great stock deal, and he talked me into spending a fair amount of money on a high-risk, but sure, bet. As you can imagine, I naïvely put the money in and lost it all within the month. I came to learn that all the while, he knew the stock was going to go bad, and I was going to lose a lot of money. He took advantage of me, and after this happened, I couldn't help but think of that poor frog and how stupid he was for allowing the scorpion to hitch a ride. I quit beating myself up and took the parable to heart. Subsequently, he kept trying to get together with me again, to hook me into another "sure bet." He tried all the tricks, "Let's go skiing" and "Let's go for a run." With compassion in my heart, I had to take a lesson from the Bible (Romans 16:17) to "mark and avoid" him, as he was a scorpion.

If it's in someone's nature to purposely cause us pain, we can't do anything about it. Worse, they may not even realize they are doing it, or the extent to which their actions hurt us. The best we can do is to make like a frog and hop away and refuse to be stung.

I sometimes think about Brian Banks, the NFL prospect who was wrongly accused of rape by a classmate when he was 16. He insisted he was innocent but accepted a plea deal. Five years later, the classmate admitted it had been a lie the whole time. Banks was finally free of the accusations, but he had lost five years of his life in prison. Again, the lie made it around the Internet in days. The truth came out five years later.

Missionary Charles West said, "We turn to God for help when our foundations are shaking, only to learn that it is God who is shaking them." Banks has rewired his brain and now lives a life filled with harmony and joy. His transformation started with a belief—the belief that he was not the person the media and his accuser made him out to be.

BECOME YOUR NEW MANTRA: "THINGS ALWAYS WORK OUT FOR ME."

It should come as no surprise that many people lack awareness. They are unaware of their actions, and of the short- and long-term consequences of those actions.

The result is a lack of personal leadership that may lead to compromised integrity, common sense, and ethics. Poet William Stafford says it boldly: "This is your time, your world, your pleasure." If you truly believe that this is your time, that you are here on purpose, then live with integrity and love!

If you allow others or the media to live your life, the odds are against your happiness. As my good friend, Ryan Blanck, says, "Live life on track, on purpose." Injecting self-awareness into your day-to-day life and catching and holding onto those moments on purpose is a skill.

Become your new mantra: "Things always work out for me." This may seem to some to be a "woo-woo" statement filled with fluff, but it does produce an end result. When you repeat it, this statement frames a very powerful philosophy. Remember, what you do with your time is your outer life stuff. What you do with your mind is your inner life stuff. In harmony, your time and mind can lead to a life filled with enormous purpose and meaning.

LET COMPASSION GUIDE YOU

*Live the question now. Perhaps then, someday,
far in the future, you will gradually, without
even noticing it, live your way into the answer.*

—Rainer Maria Rilke

BE THE PERSON IN THE MIRROR.

To understand better how your energy can affect others, you don't need to go all that deep. Simply think back to a time when you attended a speech or a play. Was the person giving the speech or acting in the play nervous? If so, how did this make you feel? Yes—nervous. You didn't ask to be nervous, but you mirrored their emotion. And your nervousness likely amplified theirs, making matters worse. Some believe these are your mirror neurons firing. Mirror neurons are neurons that fire both when a person acts and when the person observes the same action performed by another. The neuron "mirrors" the behavior of the other person, as though the action was the observer's own. If you can control your energy, this mirroring can be done consciously and can be very powerful.

Perhaps you are giving a speech or presentation at work tomorrow or are going to ask that special someone out on a date. Now, create the positive play or speech you want to be mirrored. Remember that if you are nervous, others will be nervous, too, and make you more nervous. You can mindfully control this with your beliefs. Connect confidence, happiness, and playfulness with your authentic objective.

Proactively doing something or sending positive thoughts and happiness to others will help you become the speech, the idea, or whatever it is. Simply put, look in a mirror and be the energy that you want to bounce back to you. You will be surprised at how powerful this "Jedi" mind trick can be in helping you fulfill your desired objective, or to move on from where you are now.

IT'S ALL ABOUT THE RESPONSE.

It's not what happens to you that matters. What matters is how you respond to what happens to you. You control the energy. How you use this belief to shape your plastic brain, keep your body's chemistry in check, and draw in energy that will serve you now and into the future is essential. Remember, what happens to you, happens to me, happens to your

---

MOVIN' ON ACTION

In your next meditation, concentrate on relaxing your mind and body and think about what you want to use your "mirror neurons" for. Write this down.

_____

_____

_____

_____

_____

_____

_____

_____

The snowflakes fall, each in their proper place."

—Zen saying

pastor, and happens to your work mates—it's called the interconnectedness of life. How you respond to what happens to you is called living. Responding positively means living well; responding negatively means living unwell. Which is that you would prefer? Ralph Waldo Emerson said, "Nothing can bring you peace but yourself."

Let's go back to our talk on bullies, liars, and thieves. I am 100 percent for justice and 100 percent for advocating for people to behave well toward one another. Wouldn't it be powerful if, even as proponents of those two things, we could also be supportive of those individuals who are doing the bullying, lying, and thievery? Instead of perceiving that they are the enemy, we could try to understand that they are suffering and deserve our compassion. What if we could all learn to respond to the bullies in a contemplative way that protects our self-esteem and personal happiness? What if we could teach people how to reframe this negative energy into an energy that channels compassion to those who need it most?

This is entirely possible, and the process is not a demanding one. I like to tell my clients to toss a prayer dart dipped in a compassion elixir at those who seem to be attempting to hurt them. This, repeated over time, sends a message that love and compassion are far greater tools than hate and hurtful words.

HEATED RELATIONSHIPS ARE NOT MEANT TO BURN.

As you manage bullies, or people to whom you gave a degree of power over yourself, it may be fun to manifest a strategy to navigate this experience better. Remember, most everything in this book is advanced through a lens of energy management; that is, it's not something you can intellectualize. As a matter of fact, if you are in your head thinking about how, what, why, when, and where, you need to get in that elevator right now, get out of your head, and descend a few floors to the gut level. As stated earlier, when you get there, slowly breathe in and out of your gut;

The problem is not that there are problems. The problem is expecting otherwise and thinking that having problems is a problem."

—*Theodore Isaac Rubin*

think of it as a smiling, happy energy being capable of making mindful decisions.

You may recall that words make up only seven percent of a human being's communication; body posture and tone of voice make up the remaining 93 percent.

Recently, I was working with an official on a building project, and this administrator kept referring to every rule, every barrier, everything I couldn't do. He truly was telling me every way I could not do the project. I consciously changed my posture and my tone of voice and sent a message of compassion from a smiling face. After all, he was probably used to dealing with a variety of different people all day long, and I was just another on his long list for the day. Within ten minutes he was talking about how he wanted to work with me and help me with the project. Moving out of my head, breathing in a new belief pattern, changing my tone of voice and posture, and embracing my true, gut-felt intention was all it took. This is fun stuff! And each of us has the power to guide how someone will respond to us!

There is a Buddhist saying: If you want to see people without problems take a tour of the local graveyard.

By holding your head up and being aware, you can teach others to see you as a confident, positive, and humble person. Getting on with your life, instead of hiding out "in your head," is a great start to seeing solutions instead of problems.

If a "friend" cheats you in a business deal or at work, it's easy to become bitter or spiteful. You might even say something spiteful or out of character, such as: "I can't believe Jim said that about me. I am so angry. When I go back to work, I'm going to tell everyone what Jim did last year."

It's so easy to think of all the things we'd like to say and play that image

MOVIN' ON ACTION

If you find yourself in a situation like the one above, try this:

Before your next negotiation or interaction with someone you perceive will be negative, go for a walk, preferably in nature. Begin by focusing on your breath. Imagine the air going in and coming out. After a few minutes, begin to become aware of your feet as they connect to the earth. Feel the wind blowing on your face. See how the tops of the trees connect to the sky and actively listen to the sounds around you. Continue walking. After about ten to fifteen calming minutes, become aware of any thoughts surrounding this charged relationship. You may see the other person in an angry space at first; observe how that makes you feel. You may be angry, as well, causing you to create mirroring neurons (which, by the way, are traveling immediately to the other person). Allow this anger to play out while you continue your walk. You may find your inner voice, giving that other person a piece of your mind. After a moment, and without hesitation, reframe your response into a positive one. Find your own statement, which resonates from your gut level. Continue your walk, allowing your inner voice to continue to reframe what your response will be. Write down that response, so that the next time you communicate with this person face-to-face, you will say something encouraging.

over and over in our minds. Perhaps it is healthy and wise to allow this movie to play out—once. Feel the emotions it brings out; anger, resentment, and hatred, etc. Keep your mind's eye on those emotions, so that

When we are unable to find tranquility within ourselves, it is useless to seek it elsewhere."

—*F. de La Rouchefoucauld*

they don't manifest pain in your body, and then rework the inner voice, gently letting them go. By the time you get back to work, you will no longer be the angry ogre.

Many of us tend to react when attacked physically or emotionally. The wise do not react; they respond.

WHAT IS THE FINE LINE BETWEEN REACTING AND RESPONDING?

What does the Japanese proverb "When you plan revenge, best dig two graves" mean? When you go after someone with the intention of causing them the same pain you felt, you may hurt them. In the process, however, you will hurt yourself again, as well. Think about your own life, or about a friend who was hurt by a relationship that went awry. Quite often it is common for the person who was hurt in the breakup process to wish ill upon the person who caused them pain. This may come in the form of a hurtful posting on Facebook or starting a rumor on a blog. These energies, manifested through the need to get revenge, are not only painful to the person upon whom you are taking vengeance, but will inject a cancer into your soul that may become permanent. Be careful of becoming the avenger and be careful to manifest only positive thoughts if people are saying or doing negative things to you.

Overcoming spiritual sadness and drain requires massive amounts of mindfulness, personal forgiveness, and affirmation. Everyone experiences this differently; how we respond truly shapes the solution to finding peace of mind and contentment.

I feel today's social media driven society lacks the old-fashioned model of forgiveness. The media trolls tend to focus in on a mistake until an individual's life/career has been ruined. For example, a person who has paid for their crime well over continues to be shunned when a simple act

Pulling someone down will never help you reach the top!"

—Author Unknown

MOVIN' ON ACTION

If there is room in your inner vocabulary to change the purpose from "revenge" to "justice" or "forgiveness," then there is room for true, authentic, meaningful action. The wisdom is in knowing the difference. The secret is to be aware that justice is about the process, while revenge is about the emotion, and forgiveness is about movin' on.

In your next meditation, choose someone who has hurt you that you could forgive. What does this Movin' On Action look like (i.e., email to the person, bringing them a plate of cookies, etc.)?

There is some truth to the saying that reason and emotion ride on the same bus. If you know something is unreasonable, you will feel strongly about it. By the same token, when you are emotional, you will invent reasons. The wisdom lies in separating the two. Is it possible that you have invented reasons to make your anger seem reasonable?

---

of forgiveness could move everyone on.

If you are thinking ill of someone, try this. In your next meditation, visualize the person you are wishing ill fighting a hard battle in some area of his or her life. Perhaps their spouse is leaving them, or they lost their

Problems cannot be solved at the same level of awareness that created them."

—Albert Einstein

job, or have some health issue you are unaware of. By being empathic, you may see them differently. The next time you meet them, try paying attention to their eyes and body language. You might intuit that they are not here to hurt you but are using you to balance their own pain. This is a very common psychological issue.

No matter what, if you practice lovingkindness, it will expand you. If this type of thinking is new to you, you may feel awkward or weird inside. I know I did. Just stay with that compassion, either in person or in your mind. Take Mother Teresa's advice and "Spread love everywhere." Any action done out of compassion can never be wasted. Even the smallest act (giving a smile, sharing a quick story, a pat on the back, a promise to pray for that person) can mean the world to someone who needs that from you.

SHOULD I EVER PUSH BACK?

Experiential mindfulness is an invitation—an invitation to go inward and/or seek some outer help like justice. As in Plato's Allegory of the Cave, you frame the form based on your beliefs or the beliefs you wish to have. How you approach each experience is the story—the chapters of your life. There is no question that if you are in a situation that requires legal or other professional advice, be wise and ask for help. Seeking justice or other professional help is a sign of strength. Using our legal or medical systems does not suggest a lack of patience or mindfulness, it is merely common sense and quite healthy. Use your mindfulness training to become aware of the most useful resources in your environment.

Here's the paradox. If you are correct, do you really need to prove anything to anyone? Again, I am not saying you should avoid using our systems and processes to get help, but when is being right just about satisfying the ego? Depending on your situation, you do not need to embody

Be kind. Everyone you meet is fighting a hard battle."

—Rev. John Watson

anger or sadness. However, you may need to accept it by using one of two mantras: "Does this experience end with me using it as a springboard to become more—to become better?" or "Does this experience require me to look outward and spend time seeking advice from others?" Regardless of which, it will always be an invitation to expand your consciousness.

Employ the available resources around you; be compassionate with yourself and others, and allow time to work its magic. And while you're pursuing the solution, be aware of how you can take this challenging moment and use it to become wiser. Can you keep your intention on a path that is moving forward, and not just a "poor me" mindset? This will truly cultivate a powerful path that is feeding the person seeking depth, substance, and culture. If you're driven by ego and win your court case, you may win the battle but lose the war. We can remain mindful of our intentions in whatever we do and keep movin' on!

MOVIN' ON: THE BOSS CHANGES, BUT LIFE GOES ON.

Jessica P. Longtine: Jessica is National Director of Life Time Kids at Life Time Fitness and a former student of mine. She has a great attitude, which really shows through in this story of how she handled a big change at work.

Once I was working for a company called Northwest Athletic Club. Life Time Fitness was their number-one competitor. They scared me, they intimidated me, and they seemed like the big dogs on the block. I went to a fitness convention and found out while I was gone my club had been taken over by Life Time.

I came back a Life Time Fitness employee. It was very, very stressful. People were getting locked out, computers were getting ripped out of the wall, and people didn't know if they were going to have a job at the end of the week. I had a whole team of people, and my people were bawling. It was their livelihood.

I did a little bit of job hunting, so I could make sure there was an out. However, I really believed that if I got my team and all of my people into a good place with Life Time, that would be best. So, instead of worrying about my own personal struggle, I poured my energies into my team and getting them to a good spot. It worked out better than one could have imagined.

At the time, it felt like the end of my career, but nearly everybody who wanted to stay made it through the transition smoothly.

What's always worked for me, truly, is to go along with it. There are company takeovers every single day. It's just jumping in—just do it. What's the worst that's going to happen?

My motto is "Always say yes before you say no." If you say no, guess what? You will never, ever in your life do a difficult yoga pose such as the side crow. But if you say yes, you might accidentally do one.

Just say, "Yeah, hey, best thing ever. I'm looking forward to this." You might surprise yourself.

SHOWING THAT YOU CARE REALLY MATTERS.

Like many of our struggles, Jessica's story isn't world-shattering. But for her, it was huge. From her experience with those that were intimidating to her, she learned to pay attention and care for her employees, even though she had no control over corporate matters. She could have taken this setback as a chance to grumble and complain. Instead, she chose to move on and got a big, national position. Choose to see the flowers!

Behavioral economist Dan Ariely did a study in which he gave a group of MIT students small amounts of money to find pairs of identical letters on a sheet of paper. He broke the students into two groups. In one group, the students wrote their names down on the paper, and the researcher diligently looked over the sheets before putting them in a pile. With the other students, the researcher did not look at the sheets, and acted as if he didn't care. Ariely discovered that the group that seemed to have

Many eyes go through the meadow, but few see the flowers in it."

—Ralph Waldo Emerson

been ignored required nearly twice as much money to keep going as the group that was acknowledged—even though the task was so simple. Like Jessica, just caring about her staff made them care about what they did. Make sure you diligently "look at the paper" for those who are important in your life.

13

BANISHING WORRY, GETTING READY FOR ACTION

FEAR IS LACK OF KNOWLEDGE.

Sometimes we don't change because we're trapped by fear and worry. Some say worry is lack of preparation. What if I told you that you could be ready for whatever comes without having to fear it? If your mind is conditioned to keep you scared and make you small, you will be a tiny, scared cat. The opposite is true, as well. The truth is, most of what an ill-conditioned brain wants you to be afraid of or worry about will never happen. Be very careful, for worrying can manifest the unknown future. When you worry about something, you put major, even neurotic energy toward what you are worrying about. This can cause a self-fulfilling prophecy and move you toward the very thing you are trying to avoid.

Harvard professor Srini Pillay says the brain has a GPS designed to direct neural tissue toward your goal. One study has shown that if you focus on an intention, as opposed to external stimuli, your brain will pull up past experiences and current opportunities, helping you to reach goals. Pillay states that setting goals is a broad action, but what's necessary for lasting change is making that goal a priority. For example, don't just let your goal be to be healthier—set up a time to exercise, choose precise foods that are healthier, and acknowledge that being stressed is what brings you back to old habits.

So how do you break this cycle and set intentional goals? We learned earlier that fear is lack of knowledge. Therefore, being fearful is optional. We have all come to learn that once we try something, we usually aren't

> ## The epitome of the human realm is to be stuck in a huge traffic jam of discursive thought."
> —*Chögyam Trungpa, Buddhist meditation master*

scared the next time we try it. Maybe, as a kid, you would never eat sushi. But having become educated by the very act of trying it, you now find it tantalizing to your tongue. Maybe you forgot this, and it's time to remember that being a beginner or being afraid about something you have no knowledge about is an illusion. Past fears or self-debilitating thoughts are there to protect you. Sorting out which past fears serve your safety and security (e.g., avoiding uncooked pork) versus those that are not real (eating raw sushi) takes mindfulness and intellect. Again, while the danger can be very real, fear is a choice. So, replace fear with imagination and set your intention on the person you're meant to become.

You may have heard that depression is living in the past, while anxiety is living in the future. If you don't want either of those, be here. Be present, right now.

One of my greatest discoveries from my own painful life experiences is that everything is temporary. A gash eventually becomes a scab, and then a scar. The snow melts, and the temperature changes. Time, combined with inner awareness, heals all wounds faster. Worry is when you forget that everything is temporary.

Over time, you will discover that your worry is simply you creating a future that doesn't need to occur. Remember, while some things are inevitable, how you respond to those things is not.

You may not always be battling big fears, but even the little ones can create barriers that keep you from living your best life. If you are out of shape, you may come to realize that you fear what you look like in public in your workout clothes, or you fear the pain of exercise. Regardless, small fears are keeping you from going to the public gym and becoming fit.

Don't fight these thoughts; rather, gently send them away and mindfully replace them with a new thought: "It's my body, not theirs, and I am going to exercise!" Again, if you fear making healthy or personal changes, find someone who will support what you want to do.

MOVIN' ON ACTION

Here's a powerful action you can take to rid yourself of a worrying, anxious mind:

Go for a thirty-minute power walk in nature to rid yourself of excess energy. Then sit down in a quiet space by a body of water. Focusing on your breath, stare into the water for ten minutes. Press your tongue to the roof of your mouth behind your top two teeth (there's a pressure point there). Breathe in through your nose for a count of four, hold it for a count of eight, and then exhale through your mouth for a count of seven. Keep staring at the water and stay with this breath play for ten cycles. Allow the water's energy to bring you to a relaxed state. If one of the things you are currently worrying about comes into your mind, become aware of it, and at that very moment visualize the worry as a bird flying by and then out of sight. Do this for any worry that pops up. When the meditation is over, keep the bird in your awareness. Every time that worry creeps into your mind, visualize the bird carrying it out of sight.

Write down a current worry you have now and draw a picture of that worry on the bird's back.

_____

_____

_____

_____

_____

MOVIN' ON: DICK HANEY

My greatest mentor, dearest friend and former boss, Dick Haney, shares his movin'-on story about his recent trip in the Canadian Quetico. Dick is nearly 80 years old and his connection to earth, his family/ friends and spirit is as authentic as it gets.

The bedrock, Canadian Shield, more than a billion years old, formed the point on the small lake where I sat, physically exhausted, with my painful feet dangling in the water, cleaning the wounds before applying ointment and bandages. This beautiful, scenic small lake at the top of a plateau was one of several also small lakes connected by brooks with barely visible and unmaintained portages providing a continuous, steep and rocky, east to west ascent from Kahshahpiwi Lake. At the western end of this nameless lake (which I now called my lake) another portage cascaded down from my high plateau lake, about 1/3 mile, to Irene, the next lake along my detour route. (An osprey suddenly dropped from above to the water with an audible splash, then immediately rose with a fish in its talons.) There were no campsites along this chain of water called the Tuck River, so I created my camp on the point where I sat, surrounded by beautiful red pine (Pinus resinosa) with a foot plus carpet of Reindeer Moss (Cladonia rangiferina), actually a lichen, which served as my comfortable mattress for the next two nights. (A loon called out and its mate answered, breaking the silence of this haven.) In this people-less Eden, totally apart from other humans, I would spend two nights, resting my weary legs and body before continuing my odyssey, before moving on. As my wounded feet were caressed by the water and the solitude of this beautiful spot consumed me, I thought about the challenges which often face us, consume us, and, sometimes drive us to concede. Sometimes that end is necessary, or wise. But, moving on, or not moving on, is a choice, usually we can find the motivation to push us on, to take some action, our limit is in the mind. The sun was sinking to the horizon, my camp had been set, my meal consumed, my hammock was welcoming me to a long night of rest, the loon family called out. There was pride within for my accomplishment that day, and promise that after a day of rest tomorrow, more challenges would face me.

Later that evening a beaver slapped its tail, startling me out of drowsiness. Was this his warning to his family? Or was he/she applauding the efforts of this old traveler, congratulating me, or, perhaps, encouraging me to get off his stage where few humans ventured? The temptation to rest yet another day tugged at my mind.

There are times in our lives when it would be easy to concede to such temptation, perhaps times when we should, and times when we do. For several reasons it seemed necessary to move on. (The pair of trumpeter swans that just descended to the water tested my commitment to move on. There were no young with them; they did not serenade me with their Sousa-like bugle call).

I loaded the canoe and paddled to the portage. Another day which would become strenuous began. The portage demands were lessened by my decision to carry some of my "not-needed now" gear across late on the previous rest day, lighter loads across this first portage. Several portages and several miles later on this warm, sunny day tested my endurance. Then came the end of a lake with two options (two portages) starting as one path for 100 yards then deviating, each providing routes through different lakes, then eventually converging to a common route several miles to the south.

My Canadian maps were not topographic, no contour lines, no hints to the elevation changes of each route. I would learn by experience that my choice provided significant elevation change, and I started on the low end of the portage. I carried my canoe across for the first part of my triple portage routine, my transportation vehicle was the most precious—a necessity, deserving of the freshest effort across.

Within a few hundred yards, I discovered that the trail went straight up a steep, rocky climb for as far as I could see. The footing was treacherous, and the effort to ascend was draining my strength, affecting my balance and control. "Just keep moving." At the top of several tops of the trail, the land descended a shorter distance, but just as steep, to the shore of the next lake. Two more trips across, perhaps this would require 4 total crossings with a further division of the remaining loads. Descending the hill in my return for load two, I grimaced in dread of the need to climb this "peak" two or maybe three times more.

Trip two was one heavy pack. Using arms and hands to grab trees and boulders assisted my legs up the slope. I told myself, "Don't look up to see how far it is to the top. Focus on each step, a good place to step, a tree or rock to leverage each step." One foot in front of the other, the end will announce itself, each step is a goal. The return for crossing three involved a self-debate: carry the two remaining packs, one large and the other smaller, both in a third crossing? Or do four trips? The

See into life, don't just look at it."

—Anne Baxter

thought of descending that slope one more time drove me to the decision to carry the two packs together—one load.

Could my legs and body find the strength to reach the top? At the base of the incline, I decided to load the large pack on my back, go up a step or two, reach back with a hand and pull the small pack up to and beyond my position. Repeating this process again and again, honoring my vow to not look up for the crest, like a caterpillar I ascended to the top. (How I wished I could yodel!) After a few moments of rest, I began the descent, cautiously, to my destination a final time, with no need for a fourth trip.

About two hours later, my last backpacks joined the other pack and the canoe. After a snack and water were consumed, the canoe was loaded and the float down the next lake proceeded. The goal that I had doubted was possible to reach ... was reached. The body and mind, which were depleted, were not. Through the fog in my mind and the physical fatigue, a motivator was found that pushed me on. Movin' on, one footstep after another, one paddle stroke after another, the end would be in sight in the next 4 or 5 days. Life moves on whether or not we do. So, be sure to take the time and to focus on the "flowers" along the way. Life is more than moving along, it is keeping a focus on a goal while enjoying the sensory stimulations which enrich our experiences.

THE SKILL OF SELF-DIRECTION.

Self-direction is the ability to observe your debilitating thoughts, actions, and behaviors without judgment, and then consciously change them so you think, act, and feel the way you want to. One of my best friends is an alcoholic. He says we are all addicted to one thing or another, and how we respond to that addiction, big or small, shapes our happiness. There are many definitions of addiction, but for him, it's simple: you are repeatedly doing something you or a loved one knows is hurting you and/or those you care about.

Lately, I have been noticing myself going on social media more than I want. The funny this is that I realize it but I don't do anything about it.

MOVIN' ON ACTION

If this is you, try observing yourself hovering over your body. Don't cast judgment, and certainly don't beat yourself up. Simply become aware and watch yourself doing what you do not want to do. After a few minutes of this observation exercise, start imagining yourself performing an action you would rather be doing.

What are you addicted to? What actions are you taking to overcome it?

_____

_____

_____

_____

_____

_____

I get frustrated when I realize I just blew two hours looking at the Facebook news feed. I don't want to waste this time, but I do. Yes, this is an addiction.

For example, instead of being on Facebook, I could see myself writing in my journal or exercising. Try the Movin' On Action on the next page. When you're done observing, listen. Listen to your inner voice saying, "Check Facebook." Capture that voice and reframe it to say, "You don't have to check Facebook. Read a book or a magazine—it's healthier." After a while, you will retrain your mind to teach your brain to act out what you really want to do. As an aside, this is just one example of the many areas I need to work on. You are not alone!

14

YOUR AUTHENTIC YOU

BE IN THE MOMENT, NOT ON A SMARTPHONE.

The first part to reinventing yourself is gaining a better understanding of who your authentic self really is. For me, being entrepreneurial, keeping fit, making those I care about a priority, being playful, staying connected to the natural world, and building community are just a few things that define my authentic self. To feed this authentic self, I make it a point to do something creative, exercise daily (preferably in nature), and be with friends and family as much as possible.

I had a fitness instructor many years ago who struggled to find friends and be accepted in group situations. She was a straight-A student and physically healthy but acted as though she wasn't smart. One day she came to my office and asked me why no one ever took her seriously, and why she didn't get invited to social events with the other instructors. When I gently shared the insight with her that she was teaching the people, via her behavior, that she was uneducated and irritating—two things she truly was not—she left my office in a huff. A few years passed, and one day she showed up at my office in a professional business suit, carrying herself with a confident posture, and radiating success and contentment. She said that what I told her years ago had given her pause to reflect. Upon graduating and moving to a new city, she decided to reinvent herself. She was the number-one salesperson at her job, had a great husband, and was eager to take on the challenges of the world. She had truly reset her mind, and ultimately, her life. Remember, unhappiness can be defined in many ways, one of which is that you are being

The way to make your dreams come true is to wake up."

—Paul Jackson

someone that you don't want to be or are not doing something you know you should be doing. Ralph Waldo Emerson said, "You become what you think about all day long."

How could you possibly be happy if you think about negative things all day long?

YOU CAN REINVENT YOURSELF.

The Bible says that you reap what you sow. If you plant good thoughts, good thoughts will grow. There's an action-response cycle. Similarly, in Buddhism, the lotus flower blooms and bears fruit simultaneously representing the oneness of cause and effect. In short, when we plant a good thought (i.e. cause) concurrently, we pave the road to a positive effect in the future that may or may not be obvious.

The wise can easily discern and conclude that the best way to live a happy life is to manifest good thoughts as much as possible.

Your limitations are self-imposed, and this self-imposition, which usually stems from childhood fears or events, can be brought back to the surface by current traumas or life-changing events that occur in your adult life. Entrepreneur and author John Assaraf says, "A thought cannot experience … it can only make up, create, and interpret. It needs a world of relativity (the physical world, body) to experience self."

DON'T ALWAYS TRUST YOUR INTUITION.

Don't always trust your intuition, especially if you are fatigued or in a deep emotional imbalance. There's a general rule-of-thumb in the wellness world. That rule is to know that your balanced mind cannot handle more than six major decisions at a time. For example, buying a car could be one such major decision. There are many other big decisions: buying a house, breaking up with your spouse/significant other, losing your job, getting a new job, your child having problems in school, your child looking at colleges, etc. If you practice observing yourself, you will become aware whether or not your bucket of decisions is overflowing. In this moment, when you are overstuffed with life's mind-consuming details, be careful when listening to your intuition. At this point, your subconscious is in panic mode, and, in the process of seeking balance, it may drive your decision-making mechanism to act hastily. If that is the case, make a conscious decision to hold off on adding new decisions to your repertoire until the energy of the current decisions have subsided.

Over time, the "car" and/or "house" decisions will go away, and you will find balance in your current thought load. Again, movin' on, or to-ward, your authentic self is about waking up to what is causing your neurons to fire and turning the steering wheel toward your purpose. You can control your response—it is time to start believing that (if you are not already doing so)!

MOVIN' ON ACTION

Try this if you are feeling overwhelmed: Be with this feeling in your next meditation. Gently observe your mind, and how it is responding to both large and small decisions in your daily life. Then decide, in positive terms, how you will slow down, breathe, and respond to life's decisions consciously and wisely. Write down what major decisions you have on your plate right now, and how you are going to manage them.

Note: If you have more than six big decisions in your life, write down how you are going to say no to adding more.

_____

_____

_____

_____

_____

One further thought on emotions: If you've ever had an x-ray, your x-ray technician probably put a lead pad on the part of your body that was not being examined to prevent wandering x-rays from causing any damage. Emotions can be like that lead pad, but in an unhealthy way. The bigger the emotions, the more they cover up your awareness and prevent your ability to think clearly. If you can be mindful of these emotions, you can remove the lead pad.

My good friend, Charles Wolf, competes in world-class ultra-distance kayak races. His latest race was a three-hundred-mile-plus race around the southern tip of Florida. I was speaking with him about the race, and he shared with me something the wise race director, whom everyone referred to as "Chief," told all the athletes at the starting line. "Chief told us that there will be a point in the race where you will, without question, want to quit. But before you quit, promise me that you will do this: go to the beach, drag your boat up on shore, set your tent, and get a good night's sleep. When you wake up, eat a good breakfast, enjoy the sunrise, and then—and only then—decide if you'll drop out or keep on going."

Charles followed this advice during a heavy storm. The storm picked up steam, and, due to the high waves, he went up on shore. It was cold and wet, and, even though he was only a few hours into the race, there was no question he was going to drop out. But he had promised to take the Chief's advice. After a good night's sleep, the sunrise, and a good cup of coffee, Charles moved past his limitations. Not only did he go on to finish the race, he finished third overall in his class.

Patience will give you the needed time and renewed energy to make the right choice to reframe your thoughts toward an intuition based on sound mind and sound body. I'm reminded of motivational speaker Wayne Dyer's famous quote, "When you change the way you look at things, the things you look at change."

Another example: If you are a smoker, you could set your belief on being a "nonsmoker." Then sit with that image. See yourself after a meal, having a drink, stressed out at work, going for a long walk, thinking of your kids, etc. What patterns subconsciously trip you to grab a cigarette, and which ones don't? Be with those triggers and become aware of the fears you're feeling. What action could you do to overcome those fears? Can you get up and go for a walk? Drink some water? Focus on the clean, clear air entering your lungs, cleansing out all the black, gooey tar? Think of your kids and how they will be so happy that you will live longer? Think of the money you're saving? Now, mindfully live this non-smoker's reality.

If our mind truly believes that a particular behavior or goal is something it wants to learn, then our brain will direct our physical body in that direction. When I attended a training camp for cycling some years ago, the Olympic coach had us all do a cool activity to test our beliefs. He lined up all of us athletes behind a white line. I looked down the line at the thirty cyclists, wondering what the coach had up his sleeve this time.

Then he said, "Today we are going to do the broad jump!"

I thought to myself, *What the heck is this going to do to improve my cycling?*

He said that this was a special broad jump, as the person who jumped the farthest would get a massage and extra dessert after dinner. Immediately, we all became super-hyper-competitive. He gave the countdown: one … two … three … jump! We all launched ourselves as far as we could. He told us to stay standing where we'd landed. We assumed he was going to measure our jumps to select the champ. Instead, he came by with a bucket of stones, and proceeded to give each of us a stone.

"Don't move!" he said. "This stone is magic. It has the ability to give you strength, to allow you to go farther than you could ever have imagined."

We were perplexed. What was our coach trying to say, here?

"Take this magic stone and place it six inches in front of your feet," he said. "I know you all believe you jumped as far as you possibly could. But this stone will prove whether that was true."

Leaving our stones six inches past where our feet had been, we moved back to the white line.

"Now look at the stone and believe you can. One … two … three … jump!"

I couldn't believe it. We all jumped to the stone! Most of us jumped past it. He told us each to take our stone and keep it with us whenever we lacked faith in ourselves. I never forgot that lesson, and I often draw on that energy. It's not just about physical competition. Rather, it was a gentle reminder that we do not always reach our limits—and, moreover, that we usually don't even know what they are.

MOVIN' ON ACTION

Here are five quick steps you can take right now to move past your limitations:

1. Knowing that your beliefs become your mental image of yourself, set a belief on something you want to change, such as exercising more, and then see that image in your mind's eye (e.g., get up to exercise before work).

2. Sit with this image for a while, and see what fears arise (e.g., having to go to bed early, missing out on fun, experiencing the pain of exercise, being too tired, not having enough time, etc.).

3. Once you become aware of those fears, determine what you need to learn or to believe to overcome them (e.g., "You'll have more energy for the day if you go to bed earlier, and then get up early to exercise." "Start out easy, and the exercise won't be painful.").

4. Take some form of action to overcome that fear (e.g., call up a friend and ask them to join you, hire a coach, or whatever—take the first step).

5. As you are living the aforementioned steps, truly feel how this becomes your reality (e.g., smile and enjoy the process, let go of results, become an early riser who exercises wisely).

All truths are easy to understand once they are discovered; the point is to discover them."

—Galileo

MOVIN' ON ACTION

Here's a powerful contemplative exercise you can try:

Go to the nearest graveyard and just begin walking around. Look at the gravestones and ask yourself, "How many of these folks took their great idea, that one opportunity, or that desire to say, 'I love you' to that special someone, to the grave?" Why did they not do these things before dying, and how does this resonate with you? Are you jumping as far as you can?

_____

_____

_____

_____

_____

_____

_____

_____

_____

15

TAKE A CHANCE.

To dare is to lose one's footing momentarily.
Not to dare is to lose oneself.

—Søren Kierkegaard

I used to run an adventure school for kids. I would take them rock climbing, canoeing, backpacking, and biking. This was a program for targeting "low-income youth at risk." I hated that label. I would question it often and would ask the program director to change the name to "Youth should be taking risks." Encouraging kids (and adults) to take good risks, particularly those found in the natural world, is healthy. We all know that kids will take risks; it's in their genes.

One day my co-leader, Jill, and I were preparing for an overnight trip with twelve kids at a remote campsite at Jay Cooke State Park, on the outskirts of Duluth, Minnesota, when a radio warning alerted us: "Attention all Duluthians, please be warned that two convicts have shot a police officer and are on the run. They were last spotted in West Duluth." (about five miles from where we were going to be camping). Of course, we had already planned the trip, the kids were excited, and the parents had already signed the waiver, so the responsibility fell on Jill and me … who, at 19 years of age, just wanted to have fun. So, we proceeded to go camping.

Everything was going great. We got the campsite set up, the food cooking, and the kids laughing. Then, Raymond, a portly redheaded 13-year-old, said, "My cousin said we are going to be taken hostage tonight by two guys who broke out of jail. Is that true?" Of course, Jill and I did what any good group leaders would do. We lied.

"There's no one else out here, Raymond. Get back to gathering wood, and after we set up camp we're going to go down to the river and check out the bat migration." All was well. We finished our dinner, told a few stories, and waited for the night sky to darken completely.

The time came to hike down to the river and check out the bats. It was a warm but eerie night. The fog was rolling in. We shone our flashlights over the river, and you could see thousands of bats flying inches above the water, eating every insect in sight. It was freaky—and, on top of it all, there was a weird kind of silence throughout the forest. Jill finally broke the ice and said in a whisper, "Do you think those two murderers are out here and are waiting to take one of us hostage?"

"I don't know," I responded. "But it's definitely a possibility. Let's head back up to camp where we're all together." So, we told the kids that it was time to head back. They were not happy.

Then it happened.

As we made our way back up the sandy riverbank toward the campsite, I looked down and my heart dropped—fresh boot marks! I walked a little farther, and there were some fresh human feces. We were in a deep, remote campsite. No one else was within miles of us, and we were in grave danger. I quickly showed Jill, and her face turned as white as snow. Trying to keep the calm, I playfully shouted at the kids that we needed to head up to the campsite right now, before the bats got trapped in their hair. That was all it took to get them, including Raymond, to run full-steam back up to camp.

I kept the fire roaring like a pick-up truck and stayed up all night holding a big stick. Fortunately, the convicts never entered our campsite, but I knew for a fact that they were there and thought about whether they might grab one of us.

How you respond to life's experiences—both on the prevention side, as well as the reaction side—has two very different energies. In this case, we never should have gone in the first place—and, moreover, once we saw the tracks and other signs of danger, we should have left the site and returned home to safety immediately. However, the sense of adventure overtook our common sense and concern for safety. Be careful not to err too many times on the side of compromised safety and common sense— eventually, you will lose.

The good news is, we got a great story out of it, and occasionally, when I bump into one of the kids, I tell them the inside scoop, and I always get a laugh.

We should consider every day lost on which we have not danced at least once. And we should call every truth false which was not accompanied by at least one laugh."

—Friedrich Nietzsche

Taking chances also applies to other areas of life, like competition. My Olympic cycling coach once told me that to win you must first risk losing. I am not sure he was the first to say that, but it has stuck with me ever since. In cycling, if you are not a good sprinter, a good strategy may be to attack with ten miles left in the race (the sprinters usually start with one or fewer miles to go). If you want to win, you need to risk all your energy, hoping that the good sprinters will lack the endurance to be able to stick with you. If they catch you, you will surely lose. It's the same in the restaurant business, in relationships, and in deciding whether or not to have kids. You can be certain that you will never win the race you don't sign up for. Winning is signing up. You can be a winner right now, if you simply overcome the fear of losing.

My former employee, Jessica Rossing, has the habit of living out loud. Recently, she went to Cuba to participate in a triathlon. The country had just opened to Americans, and she would be one of the first to race in this beautiful place. As with all travel, there were risks involved in going there by herself, but that did not stop her. Not only did she win the race, but USA Today also featured her and the other Americans in a story that hit the Internet by storm.

Start saying, "I'm in," and allow these new experiences to shape your mind into that of a fun person filled with confidence, culture, and positive stories. After all, when you are holding that walking cane near the end of your life, all you will have are the stories. Make some good ones now!

TAKE A CHANCE.

YOU WILL ALWAYS GET RESULTS

Many of our learned beliefs convince us that "knowing" and "being right" matter. It's hard for our ego to say we changed our mind, because that is proof that we were wrong before. But just because we're able to learn from the scars we receive, doesn't mean we were wrong in the first place. Quite often people who have experienced something negative end up beating themselves up. Their self-deprecating behavior has them in a space where they feel that they needed to "learn their lesson." Rather than wallowing in this ineffective belief, meditate on the freedom you've obtained by making peace with your newfound knowledge. See yourself as gaining experience versus failing. The experience does not have to control or sway you from your authentic self.

Be careful not to make false promises with your inner voice. It is common that some people who have been in an emotional situation, such as a drinking-and-driving violation, or some other unethical behavior, will say something silly like, "I will never, ever drink again"—or, worse, "I will never make a mistake again"—only to make that (or some other) mistake the next day. We are human, we have shortcomings, and we will miss the boat. Understand that some of God's greatest gifts are received through "missing the boat."

However, as American scholar Joseph Campbell states in his famous narrative, *The Hero's Journey*, our lives are a series of events, albeit different for each and everyone one of us, that follow a predictable and sequential pattern. Like all movies, stories, dramas, and plays, the journey (or story) more or less plays out like this:

1. The hero is introduced in his ORDINARY WORLD, like Luke Skywalker in the desert in the opening scene of *Star Wars*.

2. Then, the hero receives the CALL TO ADVENTURE, like Luke Skywalker being asked to go save the universe.

3. The hero is then RELUCTANT to take on this adventure and has to be coerced or forced to take action, like Luke Skywalker going back to the desert only to find his family has been killed.

4. Then the hero CROSSES THE FIRST THRESHOLD where he eventually encounters TESTS, ALLIES, and ENEMIES. Like Luke Skywalker at the bar meeting Han Solo, and they leave on the journey to save the universe.

There are only two or three human stories, and they go on repeating themselves as fiercely as if they had never happened before."

—Willa Cather

5. The hero, at some point, reaches the INNERMOST CAVE where he endures the SUPREME ORDEAL, like Luke Skywalker in the garbage smasher where he is grabbed by the monster and almost dies.

6. After the miraculous recovery, the hero eventually finds the treasure and begins his challenging ROAD BACK to his world.

7. The hero is RESURRECTED, and the experience of it all fully transforms him into a new man, like Luke Skywalker becoming a mature Jedi.

8. After all of this, the hero RETURNS to his ordinary world a new man who can positively impact the world.

So, as in the narrative above, all of our lives follow this storyline, and we are subject to the magic of the hero's journey. Remove the Hollywood element and let's look at this in another way. Bottom line, the hero's journey is about the transformation of self. To become the hero, you have to squeeze through the crucibles life brings. In other words, in order to have a meaningful life and extraordinary things, tough times are a prerequisite. Let's take the examples of the alcoholic or the unfaithful spouse. Can they emerge heroes? Will they ever enjoy the true treasures that life has to offer?

Let's play out the Joseph Campbell steps above for the person struggling with life due to alcohol.

1. The alcoholic's ORDINARY WORLD consists of day in and day out drinking, missing work, unhealthy relationships, etc.

2. Eventually, the alcoholic receives the CALL TO ADVENTURE from a friend inviting him to a 12-step program or the like.

3. The alcoholic is then RELUCTANT to go to the 12-step program until he receives his second DUI and is forced to go there.

4. In the 12-Step program, the alcoholic CROSSES THE FIRST THRESHOLD where he meets his sponsor who challenges him, encour-

── **MOVIN' ON ACTION** ──

What is your crucible?

_____

_____

Who are your mentors?

_____

_____

Are you open to full transformation? Will you take the chance?

_____

_____

_____

ages him, and tests him.

5. Over time, he reaches the INNERMOST CAVE where he endures the SUPREME ORDEAL, where he slides back and goes on a binge drinking session and nearly dies.

6. After the miraculous recovery, the alcoholic eventually finds the truth, quits drinking, and begins his challenging ROAD BACK to mending broken relationships, regaining health, and holding down a job.

7. In a few years, the alcoholic is RESURRECTED and, through the experience, fully transforms into a new man.

8. In the end, the alcoholic RETURNS to his ordinary world (family, work, old friends) a new man who can positively impact the world.

What is important to note is that if the alcoholic doesn't follow these stages and instead takes up drinking again, he will be thrust back into step 5 where he may eventually die (metaphorically or literally).

16

JOY = SERVING OTHERS.

My life is my message.

—Mahatma Gandhi

I have colleagues and family who get up in the morning, drink a pot of coffee, go to work, watch TV, party on the weekends, and repeat. Is this a meaningful life? Is this happiness? The question spiritual teachers have been asking since the beginning of time is this: "What in the heck are you here for?"

Do you feel like your life is a farce, at times … like you are pretending? Do you ever feel this weird sense of inauthenticity? You are not alone. I have felt this way, and, at times, I still do. The great spiritual teacher, Rick Warren, says the world's definition of happiness is "looking good, feeling good, and having the goods." He argues that true happiness is "being good and doing good." He goes on to say that it's not status, sex, or salary that brings true joy, but serving others.

YOUR PASSION IS NOT NECESSARILY YOUR VOCATION.

Matt Evans: One of my dearest friends, Matt Evans, who is a physics

professor, taught me about the work-life balance. For him, finding this balance was circular and required patience.

In my late teens and early twenties, I was going to school and working out. I defined myself through running and triathlons, filling my free time with wonderful friends, working at a bike shop for parts, and living for the next race. I founded a wonderful triathlon-training program, with Rod Raymond, and saw this as a calling, leading people to get in shape and enjoy being healthy. At 25, I had a decision to make: Do I follow my passion to train and continue to define myself through sport, or do I go to graduate school in physics? I realized that doing both would marginalize one at the expense of the other. The anguish of leaving behind a lifestyle that filled me with joy and camaraderie for one that demanded long hours, self-sacrifice, and common set-backs was daunting. It would have been easy to stay the course, to settle in to a lifestyle that had fallen into my lap—but I loved running and triathlons and all the friendships to the extent that I wanted to separate them from my career.

I wanted to follow a path that challenged me, that allowed me to move into a life that would lead to personal satisfaction. I chose physics, which led me to an amazing teaching career filled with both success and setbacks, fulfillment in vocation, and a sense of serving society. Fast-forward twenty-five years, and I find myself migrating back to my former life—but on my terms.

My hobby of running and triathlons has expanded beyond merely participating in them. I realize that I can help others cultivate their passion, leading to a new level of personal fulfillment. By putting on races and offering half-marathon running classes, I am able to relive my early twenties, but from the perspective of an older, less competitive athlete. I never left the world of working out, but now I am coming back to it in order to foster and share my passion with others.

YOUR CAREER DOESN'T NEED TO BE YOUR PASSION.

Matt once told me, "It's an illusion that you have to live your dream job."

Over the years, I shared his advice with hundreds of students. They would often come to my office and say, "I love fitness, and I want to be an adult fitness instructor."

My reply was usually, "Wait, what do you love second-most?"

They were usually perplexed by my question. I would then say, "Why not study to become a counsellor or for another career that you'd always thought would be meaningful, and teach yoga two times a week to fulfill your passion?

We have been told to chase the dream of the perfect job. Do you have to make money at what you love doing? Or can you find something else that you like well enough to pay the bills? Make sense? When talking to those who are planning on going to college, encourage them to explore

---

MOVIN' ON ACTION

How are you serving others? Write down three things you're doing now.

1. _____

   _____

2. _____

   _____

3. _____

   _____

---

career options that are fruitful and meaningful, and to participate in extracurricular activities that feed their passions. In my fitness example, many of my past students who took my advice went to work in the fitness industry. And many of them ended up wearing a suit and tie, pushing numbers, and counting dollars instead of promoting health anyway. The key is to find something interesting. The joy will follow.

JIM MORRISSEY: DARING TO LIVE IN THE FACE OF DEATH

My boyhood mentor, Jim Morrissey, who recently passed away, was my hockey coach, my second father, my mentor, a decorated Korean Army vet, and all-around great guy. Years ago, we named our youth fitness foundation after him: the Jim Morrissey Youth Fitness and Adventure Foundation. The story of his survival during the Korean War is one of the most powerful I've heard in my life.

A few years back, Jim and I were kayaking the Apostle Islands on Lake Superior when he stopped me and said, "Rod, I need to tell you a story that I haven't told anyone, not even my wife." He proceeded to tell me a story that forever changed my idea of who he was. It's a story that shows brotherly compassion, dedication, and bravery in the face of death—movin' on in the truest sense.

It was the dead of winter, we were fighting in North Korea. My company was ordered to protect a hill right above a frozen rice paddy the size of a small Minnesotan lake. Every twenty to thirty minutes, small groups of North Koreans, dressed in white, looking like ghosts, would come across that paddy firing their guns in full strength. We were able to hold them off all day, but things turned when night came. Because we couldn't see, we would have to fire flares in the air to light

up the rice paddy. We had a limited number of flares, and we figured we could fire one every thirty minutes and make it through the night. I remember it being so cold that I couldn't feel my hands or feet. If I were to take off my boots to warm my feet, I would surely die if we had to get out of there fast.

We fired flares all night and all seemed calm. Then, about three in the morning, we fired a flare in the pitch-black sky, expecting to see nothing. To the shock of our weary eyes, the field was filled with hundreds of these ghostly men, and they were rapidly floating directly toward us. They began shooting, and it just didn't stop. My buddies were getting shot left and right. There was nothing we could do. I looked over the hill and took inventory. Twenty-two of the twenty-five of us were dead. I yelled down to my captain, who was forty feet below me in a foxhole with a young private: "We need to retreat immediately!" I looked down and they weren't moving. I could see they were alive, but not running up to me. I yelled again. Still no movement. So, I left my bazooka and the protection of my foxhole, and belly-crawled down to them.

When I arrived, the most powerful thing that has ever happened in my life occurred. I yelled at the captain with bullets flying by: "We need to leave now!"

He agreed and yelled to the other man, "Private, for the last time, grab your stuff and we need to leave now!"

The private was frozen in shock. With the enemy less than a quarter mile away, the urgency was rapidly increasing. I screamed at him, "We need to leave now, private!"

At that point, I looked over and everything happened as if in slow motion. The private looked at me with his 18-year old eyes and slowly collapsed. He was dead. It wasn't a bullet, nor was it a hand grenade. He just died. At the time, I didn't have a clue what had happened. To this day, I believe it was fear that killed him. The private was so scared that his brain took the most massive action it was capable of—it killed him.

We had no option but to say a short prayer and run like crazy. As we ran, we decided to split up; the captain went one way and I went the other. In the process, I was shot in the hand, splitting it wide open. I didn't have time to feel the pain, my mind was saying one thing: Run!

I spent the next three days under a bridge eating the last of my rations, while watching three-thousand-plus North Korean troops walk over me. When the coast was clear, I abandoned my bridge hideout and ran toward the American medical location. I figured it was more than fifteen miles away, and with the enemy right there, my gunshot wound, frozen feet, and no food, making it out alive was a long shot. I began to run and run.

As I ran, to my surprise, I noticed my captain at the side of the same road. He had been shot in the leg and was unable to run. Without hesitation or reservation, I picked up the captain, despite his orders to leave him, put him over my shoulder, and began hiking. Whenever I heard an enemy vehicle I would dive into the ditch, covering his mouth to mute his screams of pain. We continued our journey, never believing we weren't going to make it. Unlike the private, by the end of the fourth day, we made it to safety. We are best friends to this day.

I believe Jim's scars were symbols of his strength. His totally deformed hand, where he'd been shot, is etched in my mind forever. He never complained. After all, the scar means the wound has healed and the pain is gone. It is no surprise that the giants of this world, from Mother Teresa to the most successful business people, are seared with scars, and some of those scars are usually from serving others.

As Joseph Campbell stated in his book, *The Hero's Journey*, they've learned the fine art of movin' on. Fear is a very powerful emotion. Be careful of living in it. Remember, danger is real, but fear is an illusion—just breathe, set the intention to be aware of your fear, and live your authentic self, in this moment, to the best of your abilities, like Jim did.

17

THE PROCESS IS WORTH IT.
STAY THE COURSE.

THERE IS ALWAYS A PRICE TO PAY,
AND IT IS USUALLY WORTH IT!

A s a serious athlete, during the racing season, I missed the parties on Friday and Saturday nights because I had to get up early the next day to train or to run a race. My successful musician friends say they spend ninety-five percent of their time playing in their basements, not in front of the crowds. Think of that the next time you're listening to a good musician: That two-hour set where everyone is going crazy cheering for them is the result of three hours of practice every day for years.

As a craft beer restaurant and yoga studio owner (Fitger's Brewhouse and Evolve Duluth), I can assure you that while it is still fun to drink a good ale with my friends in my own place and to help people achieve optimal wellness, the early years were spent burning the midnight oil, crunching numbers, and managing people.

This is not to say that it wasn't worth it. My musician friends wouldn't change a thing. The sound of their fans singing their songs back to them brings a level of happiness few will ever experience. The feeling I get when someone has an extraordinary experience at one of my restaurants, my yoga studio, or one of my seminars is truly wonderful. The feeling of winning a race is the highest level of elation, and it's the result of focused effort repeated over time.

SUCCESS RESULTS FROM A FOCUSED
EFFORT REPEATED OVER TIME.

There's no question that the process is what makes it fun. For the great athlete, the rock star, or the good mom, the process has its ups and downs. The rock star plays the guitar all day, struggling to get that riff just perfect. The athlete pushes his or her body just beyond its limits to increase performance. And the parent nurtures his or her children day in and day out, in the hope that they become happy, productive adults. When the journey is far more fulfilling than the destination or finish line, you have reached flow, and the neurons in your mind are setting the stage for continued mastery. In all that you do, cultivate that mastery every day, and the fruit of that healthy mindset will bring you joy beyond your wildest imagination. When it comes to others you know who are on the journey chasing wild dreams, reflect on what Amelia Earhart said: "Never interrupt someone doing something you said couldn't be done."

THE MORE TIME WE SPEND ON SOCIAL MEDIA,
THE MORE INADEQUATE WE MAY FEEL.

We live in a time of massive distraction, and sticking to goals and dreams until we reach the finish line is becoming increasingly more difficult. With the non-stop pinging of smartphones and a myriad of screens everywhere we go, there's no wonder business leaders are struggling to find employees who can stay on task and get the job done. Social media is more powerful than anything we have ever experienced. It triggers both biology ("She liked my post, therefore, she thinks I'm sexy") and curiosity ("I have to check my news feed to see what all my friends are doing—don't want to miss out"). My guess is that most people don't seem to recognize this power and how it shapes their mindsets. As I mentioned earlier, managing the distraction quotient (DQ) should be taught at every school in the Western world. For you, it should become a part of your daily contemplative practice. I know my inner mind and outer time management abilities are constantly being challenged by the inescapable smartphones, media spin, and endless other distractions happening each minute I am awake.

PUT DOWN YOUR SMARTPHONE AND LIVE.

Let's keep going with this … the DQ is not a common concept, yet. Most people do not even recognize how much time they are spending being mind-blasted by social media or online clickbait. Recent research shows that the more time a person spends on Facebook, the more inadequate they feel. They see pictures of their friends in Hawaii, or skiing in Vail, and wonder why their lives are so boring. (But perhaps their friends are spending most of their time on Facebook posting photos instead of truly enjoying the moment)! When we see hundreds of people posting pictures from their expensive one-week trip, it appears as though everyone is living an adventure-filled life but us! It is unhealthy to judge what their intentions are and being happy for them and their experiences is the healthiest way to approach this. Mindfully keeping our egos and emotions in check can help us find our own experiences in our own way. Social media can trick us into doing or buying something we may not want due to our high DQ.

Spiritual writer Marianne Williamson says it best: "Our deepest fear is not that we are inadequate. Our deepest fear is that we are powerful beyond measure." Let's stop hiding from ourselves with online distractions and embrace what we have inside.

SOMETIMES WE JUST NEED TO MAKE IT HAPPEN.

There's that old Bible verse: "God causes all things to work together for good for those who love God." (Romans 8:28). If you love God and everything is blowing up around you, does that mean you don't love God enough? I am aware that this gets hard to digest sometimes but stay with that thought until you get an answer.

Here's a weird idea for you: If things are blowing up around you—your son dropped out of school, your spouse just left you, you got fired from your job, or you were recently diagnosed with cancer—try leaving this world for a while. First off, recognize that while you are having a tough experience, it's just time and space. Some physicists theorize there isn't any time or space. This theory speaks to one single universal mind or consciousness. If you want to take this to the next level, think of your dreams. Your dreams may not be in the physical world, but what if they were real? Daydreaming is the ability to consciously wonder. If I asked you to think of what bread smells like or what the warm ocean feels like, you most likely would be able to recall the smell of bread and feel the warmth of the ocean … in that moment … in that space. In other words, your dream was very real, because you really felt the ocean and smelled the bread. In short, your dreams and your thoughts do not know space or time. Imagination is a very powerful, mystical thing. Use it to go on vacation when times get tough. You can come home and deal with the issue whenever you want.

You are not alone.

We have memories that are very real, and we have dreams and ideas that come out of nowhere. Regardless, the thoughts of our friends and family are always there. Going deeper, knowing that the DNA of my ancestors is in me is very comforting. Everything they went through and learned is wrapped up in that DNA. I have unlimited access to it. I just need to find a way to tap into it.

Be careful of depending on yourself too much. The adage, "If it's to be, it's up to me," has merit when it comes to taking action; nonetheless, having the humility to know when it's time to seek help is also a great practice.

I had a friend who was a humanist. He was with me in Costa Rica once and had to leave for Nicaragua for three days. After his trip, he took the bus back home to get to work by the next morning. Later that day he called me in a panic: "The bus broke down and there isn't anyone coming. I am trying to figure out what I can do to get to my meeting on time."

GOD MADE FOOD FOR THE BIRDS BUT DIDN'T PUT IT IN THE NEST.

What was he going to do? The answer? Nothing! It was out of his hands and in the hands of a greater power. One might argue that the bus just needed to be fixed, and he's simply going to miss his meeting. My feeling is that no matter what happens to you, you are a ball of energy buzzing around this universe. For my friend, simply staying calm so his energy ball didn't get all ramped up was the healthiest thing he could do. His humanist approach, in this situation, did not offer a felt sense of security that "everything would work out," and he became very stressed. His inner voice kept screaming, "What am I to do?" However, we need to find

---

MOVIN' ON ACTION

Instead of doing your standard meditation, make this one a daydream. Go for a walk, or some other form of exercise, to get your excess energy out. Then find a calm body of water (even a bowl of water in your kitchen will work) and sit by it. Stare into the water and concentrate on your breath. After a while, bring yourself into a relaxed, dreamlike state. Once you are in this deep, dreamy place, take the experience that is blowing up around you (e.g., divorce, health problems, etc.) and insert it into your dream. Allow this painful experience to float around in this safe space. Stay with this situation for as long as you like. Now, as in the dreaming example, recognize that there isn't any time or space in this painful experience. Allow this complex, deep idea to sit with you. Perhaps your dreamlike mind changes what is going on in this ethereal world with something more positive. What happened to the "health problems" or the "divorce"? This isn't about fighting your emotions or denying that the pain is real; it is about going to an otherworldly place to explore your situation. Once you have explored it, gently come out of your meditation. Now write down what you experienced (e.g., feelings, visualizations, sounds, smells, tastes). Being able to dream pain or fear away is an awesome technique to restore functionality in this world.

---

balance. Remember what Josiah Gilbert said: "God gives every bird its food, but he does not throw it into its nest." Sometimes we get wise and realize that relying on ourselves, or even on others, is not always the best choice. Take a minute to think about trust and the bigger picture. Learning to flow with your daily work, play, values, virtues, or intuition will usually lead you onto the right path.

I was sitting next to a Canadian woman on a bus in Costa Rica traveling from Mal Pais to San José. I was making small talk and asked her what her story was.

"I packed up my stuff and hit the road," she told me. She went on to say that she wanted to learn Spanish and trying to learn it at home wasn't working.

"I'm not very good at being a beginner. I need to have a program or a class to force me to do it," she said. I thought, "What a neat philosophy." After all, being a beginner takes courage and discipline.

As a personal fitness coach for many years, I can sense when a beginner will be successful, obtaining and maintaining optimal health. I can also tell when someone is just talking and will not attach joy to exercise, good nutrition, changing sleep habits, and catching and releasing stressful thoughts. Most successful clients who want to make a change are either "sick and tired of being sick and tired," or have had some scary health issue and are determined to reach their goal. It is this kind of intensity that beginners need to embrace, to change their mindset.

PRACTICE BEING A BEGINNER.

Those who try to exercise once and listen to the toxic inner voice saying, "I stink at this," last a week or two. It is no wonder that most people who join a gym on January first are not there the following January first. I believe that to really enjoy the true treasure of life, and especially to keep movin' on, you first need to find a compelling reason and then find joy in the process. Learning to play the piano is tough. No one wants to hear you beat on the keys and teaching your fingers how to flow is not easy. Learning to surf waves is frustrating and wiping out can hurt. But if we have grit, find joy in some form or another, and stick to it, we can learn just about anything we want.

One trick to training the beginner mind is to do what my Canadian friend did, and just sign up for the class, the program, the event, or workshop. The other way is to reframe our thinking. For example, when I was learning to surf I would say, "There's not a single person out here that wasn't once a beginner like me." I would also say, "This is fun for me and them both. After all, I am providing comic relief for those on the beach watching me flail all over the place!" In the end, no one cares if you aren't good at playing the piano, surfing, or writing a book. However, they may be inspired or simply happy for you when they see you doing new things that expand the richness of your life.

Skill is attractive to people. When we're good at business, art, or music, or when we're physically fit and socially fun, people notice. The process of movin' on is faster when we are able to improve our life and diversify

Make it a point to do something every day that you don't want to do. This is the golden rule for acquiring the habit of doing your duty without pain."

—*Mark Twain*

our skill sets.

If we are good at something, and we know of others who want to learn, we should share. The traditional proverb, "He who teaches, learns the most," is so true. We will feel better sharing our skill set, and others' lives will be enriched as a result. Comedian John Foster Hall says it best: "We are all here on earth to help others; what on earth the others are here for I don't know."

Can you think of just one thing you really want to learn, which your inner voice, time, or money is keeping you from? If money is really an issue, maybe you could do something that requires time, and make that happen instead? And if you don't like doing it at first, remind yourself that you want this. You truly want to learn this skill. Make it fun!

Every year I would get students or colleagues who would say, "I really want to go to med school, but I hate the physics and cellular biology classes," or "I really want to start that business, but I really dislike doing books and marketing." There are two kinds of motivation: emotional motivation and goal-driven motivation. If you are emotionally driven, then the cell-bio class and the accounting work feels draining and painful, and you get emotional. However, if you are goal-oriented, you may simply see yourself studying two extra hours a day for fifteen weeks or spending a measly two hours a week doing books as a means toward accomplishing and living your goal. What type of person are you? After all, goals have many paths to them, and you might find that doing the books of your own business is rewarding—especially as you begin to see those numbers going up!

18

PROGRESSIVELY REALIZING YOUR GOAL

While the conscious mind writes the autobiography of our species, the unconscious mind does most of the work.
—David Brooks

When we cut ourselves or get a blister on our hand, we know it hurts. I love the cartoon "Family Guy," and the drama Peter goes through when he bumps his knee. He reaches down, feels the pain, and then proceeds to take in ten to fifteen dramatic inhales with a long breath, and then a drawn-out "Ahhhhh," on the exhale. After the last one, the joke is over, and the cartoon continues pain-free.

As a seasoned athlete, particularly in bike racing, knowing the pain won't last usually led me to better finishes. In a long bike race, it is common for individuals in the pack to "break away" and hammer off the front. If I decide to jump and go with these individuals, I will be at my anaerobic edge. My common sense tells me that I cannot sustain this speed for much longer, but my experience tells me that the others are suffering just as much as I am, and if I hang on just a little bit longer, the pace will eventually slow down.

There is a lot of truth to Robert Schuller's saying, "Tough times never last, but tough people do." As in all areas of life, the wisdom is in knowing when to go hard and when to back off.

Your consciousness is different now than it was ten minutes ago. It's always searching, molding, responding to thought. By reading and doing things that challenge us, our brains grow stronger. Managing pain is more about knowing our bodies than anything else. We know that when we whack our hand on the edge of the table, the pain will only last thirty to forty-five seconds. A child does not know this and responds with a loud scream followed by tears. By the way, I stated earlier that it is easy to distract a toddler from crying, so why are we unable to turn away from our own illusory pain? Once again, I am not saying that the pain is not real or that we should ignore it. I am saying that sometimes the pain can easily be shifted out of our brains, as with an infant, allowing us to move on or move toward something that serves us better.

LET CONSCIOUSNESS TRIUMPH OVER SUFFERING.

The ability to shift your mind from pain to no pain can be applied to your self-image, as well. When your self-image is truly seeing yourself succeed, success can be yours. I am not talking just about monetary success, but success in relationships, health, financial management, care for the earth, spiritual connections, and family.

Be careful in believing that everything happens for a reason. While it is true that everything happens "for" you, how you see this can be good or bad. When you look for a "reason," you can misinterpret the situation and be downright wrong. To think you need to change who you are or become someone else is conformity. Personal development pioneer Earl Nightingale said: "Success is the progressive realization of a worthy ideal." Indeed, those who are working toward a predetermined goal (which began as a thought) are the most successful. Those who are always questioning and changing things in their life can rarely work toward that predetermined goal.

We are social animals, not rational animals. More than half of all babies can have a deep, two-way conversation with their mothers, even at such a young age, and twins often develop their own, private "language" before they can even talk to the outside world.

How aware are we of our inner conversation? We tend to be overconfident at times. Men drown twice as often as women because their inner voice may believe, dangerously, that "Oh, I can swim this lake." One out of five men thinks he is in the top one percent of earners, and almost everyone thinks he or she is better than average at driving.

MOVIN' ON ACTION

How are you mindfully stating your goals and progressively realizing them along your journey? Write
up a list. In your next meditation, mindfully explore if
your self-esteem or self-image is hindering you from
progressively achieving your goals. If so, write down
two right now actions you can take today to overcome debilitating beliefs (i.e., negative self-talk), con-
centrating on your best qualities.

_____

_____

_____

_____

_____

_____

_____

_____

_____

_____

_____

_____

_____

Knowledge by suffering entereth."
—Elizabeth Barrett Browning

There's a big difference between the conscious and the unconscious mind. For many, the conscious mind hungers for success and prestige, but the unconscious mind just wants to be lost in its craft.

It's like when a spiritually-filled person feels at one with their source, or when one is deeply in love. Finding a healthy blend between the two mindsets is what allows us to "get stuff done," and also to find meaning in the doing. Let me say it a different way: Doing, and being with that doing, is how we truly connect to that inner communication.

Most people who fail are those who took the easy route and/or those who conformed. We all know that the most interesting folks are usually the controversial, wacky, and weird ones. For them, success is living a creative, adventure-filled life.

Think of Martha Stewart, Steve Jobs, Tiger Woods, and Mother Teresa. They all had a dream, they all manifested that dream, they all suffered some form of pain, and they all embraced the challenges and continued pursuing their dream.

If you have a dream but you conform to what others do or say, your dream may not manifest into an authentic thought driven by you yourself. If you are saying, "I am going to do this," but work toward something else instead, you are conforming. Don't beat yourself up; only one in twenty will work toward their predetermined goal. Before you begin to make excuses, note that most of the world's leaders came from poverty or have had some form of handicap.

If you are struggling to find motivation, say this to yourself repeatedly on your next moving meditation: "To believe is to succeed." This may sound trite, or like some sort of childish "You can do it," rah-rah speech—but believe me when I say that no matter where you are in life, you can rewire your brain "to believe" toward something that is better than where you are now.

BEING A GOOD PERSON

My friend Mark and I were walking the other day, and he shared a story that truly resonated with me. Many years ago, when he was in the sixth grade, he fell and hurt his back badly. He was a school crossing guard and didn't want to show any pain or fear, so he hid the pain for several weeks. He believed that if he showed any sign of weakness, he would lose his coveted job. One day while walking back to class, his back seized up so badly he fell. By the time he got back to class, he was fifteen minutes late. At that point, the teacher told the principal, and the principal, in front of the whole class, chastised Mark for being irresponsible—that his actions let the whole crossing guard force down. Mark could barely hold back the tears and said he was sorry again and again. The teacher then asked him to get up and go to the cloakroom. On his way to the cloakroom he collapsed in excruciating pain. Both the teacher and the principal jumped to his aid, called his mother, and had him rushed to emergency. Coincidently, Mark had a terrible cough that same day. At the hospital, they concluded that his cough, combined with severe back pain, meant he had tuberculosis. That day they forced him into quarantine at the sanitarium. Mark never became negative or depressed. He recalled how, once a week, all the kids would send him cards and they would call him to wish him well. He also remembers the blind man, "Willie," who would come by every day and give him candy and say things to cheer him up. It took three months for the doctors to realize that they had falsely diagnosed him, and they set him free.

Even if you think you were wrongly placed in a "sanitarium," focusing on how you can bring a more positive, healthy vibe to that space can help bring about a positive experience. Mark thanked the kids and went back to visit Willie on a regular basis. As for the evil principal and teacher, Mark doesn't even remember their names. They are long gone now.

Movin' on is the ability not to blame those who put us in a bad place. It is the ability to remember "the cards from the kids and Willie's kind words." Mark is over 60 now, and that is what has stuck with him for the past fifty years. In all areas of your life, strive to be like "Willie."

WE ARE ALL IN THIS TOGETHER.

If you have even a faint understanding of Carl Jung's *The Collective Un-conscious*, you know that all life around us has a shared consciousness. Have you ever received a call from a friend you were just thinking about? Have you ever talked about how your friend's laugh is just like a bird, and then you go outside and hear that same bird five minutes later? This is called synchronicity. The energy of your thoughts is sent out into the world, and, sometimes, the world chooses to respond. While this may be coincidental or unrelated, your mind syncs up with the event, attaching meaning. While kids mimic our actions, they also mystically tune in to our thinking.

Knowing this, we have the opportunity to positively affect kids (or those around) not only through our actions, but by our thoughts — so be very careful of what you think.

BE THE PERSON YOU
ARE MEANT TO BE

No man can get rich himself unless he enriches others.

My ultra-marathon canoe-racing friend, Charles, is a top citizen racer. He's well-known for slowing down to help a competitor in need. He realizes that life is a race, but if you don't help others in need, you are never going to win. As he said to me, "At this distance, working together makes it more meaningful and fun."

Stop thinking about all the reasons you can't be successful and start thinking about how you can. Be like Charles, measure your success by how many people you help.

Bruce Lipton said, "Every human being is equally powerful in their creative ability to shape the planet." Do you feel powerless at times? Let me state this clearly, power does not discriminate! In a healthy team, everyone is equally empowered. In conflict, ugliness stems from power inequity. That's why conflict is so much uglier than teamwork.

In the world of quantum physics nothing is solid. The things in this world, including you and me, are just big balls of energy. Many of the greatest minds agree that our thoughts are the glue that holds this dynamic field of energy together.

Our thoughts create the objects we see. So, when you are looking at your dog or fish, know that what you are really seeing is a big cluster of energy. Think of those old cartoon flip booklets. When you look at each cartoon in the booklet the picture is just a still object. However, when you begin flipping the corner of the booklet, the objects begin to move.

MOVIN' ON ACTION

Are you experiencing conflict at work or at home?

Are you the one causing the conflict due to your ego or need for power?

Or, are you the one who believes you are being over-powered?

Write down three actions using techniques thus far in this book to find resolve.

1. _____

   _____

   _____

2. _____

   _____

   _____

3. _____

   _____

Each picture in the "movie" is in a different position. In short, your eyes are playing tricks on you, and you are not seeing the reality. This is the same thing when it comes to the objects we see—the energy behind them is what's important.

A man is literally what he thinks, his character being the complete sum of all his thoughts."

—James Allen

YOUR THOUGHTS DO THE CREATING.

When we think of going to work or of creating something, we often think of our hands or our body. But regardless of what others tell us or what we may think, our body does not have the power to create. Only our thoughts have that power.

We live off the fruit of our thoughts, and the things we worked toward are gone in a split second (e.g., job, car, boat, gun, etc.). And the things we got for nothing we can never replace (e.g., the human mind, spirit, family, ideas, goals, health, etc.).

The cliché "You are what you eat," is so true. The beliefs we "eat" truly shape the people we are. We are 100 percent responsible for the harmony or lack of harmony in our lives.

Look within you—you are beyond powerful. Yes, it can be a humbling thing to do, believe me … I've been to the depths and back, only to muddle about in the space between. Harmony is a delicate dance that requires the ability to know which side of the teeter-totter needs weight to find balance.

Create your reality. You are in charge! Playwright George Bernard Shaw said, "People always blame their circumstances for what they are. I don't believe in circumstances. The people who get on in life look for the circumstances they want, and if they can't find them, they make them."

Years ago, I was in New York and watched the Broadway play *Les Misérables.* By the way, I'm the worst guy to take to a play or movie. I totally get into them. I do not want to leave a good play or movie the same person I was when I walked in, and this play was no exception. I was moved more than I ever imagined. And if I take some editorial liberties in the upcoming paragraphs, my hope is you get my point. If you've seen the play, you remember that in the beginning, the main character, Jean Valjean, a hardened man released from prison that day, is brought to stay with a gracious priest. The priest, a gentle man, gives Valjean a place to stay and food to eat. At about midnight on the first night, however, Valjean plans to steal the silver from the church and run away.

While doing so, the priest wakes up and comes to investigate. Valjean is startled, and when the priest tries to stop him, Valjean smacks him over the head with a candelabra and runs away. Later that night, the church doorbells ring, and there are two constables holding the silver and Valjean in handcuffs.

They say to the priest, who has a fresh cut on his forehead, "This silver looks like it belongs to the church, and we believe this man stole it."

The priest looks the constables straight in the eyes and says, "No that is not our silver, and I do not know this man. However, he looks like he's in need of a place to stay. Please leave him here with me."

The constables are perplexed but acknowledge the priest's wishes and leave Valjean with him. Can you imagine how Valjean must have felt?

Here's the turning point of the story. If you allow what happens next in the play to affect you the way it did me, it will change your life forever.

After the constables leave, Valjean stands there in front of the only man ever to believe in his goodness. Angry and embarrassed, Valjean asks, "Why did you do that?"

The priest looks at him and speaks these powerful words of wisdom: "Jean Valjean, the days of living your life like that are over! When they dropped you off, I didn't lie; I didn't know that man. You are not that man; you are a man of greatness, and you have the ability to do much more. Now go be the person you were meant to be." The rest of the play is filled with Valjean's greatness.

This play speaks not only to reframing your mind toward movin' on, it speaks to your ability to be like the priest and give others the space to shape their minds to become their best, most authentic selves. What a gift — to have the ability to do this for yourself as well as for others!

GOOD DEEDS.

Have you ever heard someone say, "I'm all good. Helped a guy with his car—got my good deed done for the day."?

This is a common feel-good belief. While it is good to help others, what would the world look like if you became a person who did this automatically—or, in other words, if you not only do good deeds, but become the

---

MOVIN' ON ACTION

In your next moving mediation, identify one belief you hold that is shaping a behavior you need to change. Once you identify that belief, repeat it in the rhythmic way in your next walk (in four-beat rhythm):

- *The days of living my best life have just begun*
- *The days of living my best life have just begun*
- *The days of living my best life have just begun*
- *The days of living my best life have just begun*
(repeat)

Repeating this incantation (or one of your own) daily for 2-3 weeks will rewire your brain putting in place a new belief (and thus becoming like the priest).

---

kind of person who simply thinks more about others than self? We all know someone like this—someone so filled with loving kindness, they are often referred to as an angel or a saint.

If you were to set out to become a person who thinks outside of self, you might find yourself buying two cups of coffee for no reason and giving one to a coworker. You will, without thinking about it, do your girlfriend's laundry, pick up Chinese for dinner, or pay for the person behind you in a fast food pick-up lane. It doesn't need to be the big "good deed." A mindfulness that teaches the brain to search for and act upon many small good deeds may be a mindfulness that totally changes your life around.

Have you ever observed how people respond to a beggar on a street corner? Sit back and watch it sometime. You may see folks cross to the opposite side of the street to avoid the beggar. You may see a person totally avoid eye contact. You may see a certain kind of ashamed body language awkwardly shooing the beggar away. In short, you will see people who want neither to see the beggar themselves, nor be seen by others saying "No!"

MOVIN' ON ACTION

In your next meditation, create a space in your mind that reframes your thoughts to think about others.

Write down three good deeds you could do for a co-worker, family member, and friend in the coming days.

1. _____

_____

2. _____

_____

3. _____

_____

IS COMPASSION SELFISH?

Back in the Stone Age, if you didn't help out a fellow clan or tribe member, you would not receive help when you needed it yourself. In other words, you helped the person out solely in the hope that they would help you out next time—a selfish gesture necessary for survival. Moreover, you needed to be seen doing so by other members of your tribe. If others saw you, they might also be ready to help you out in the future. Perhaps the motivation for this archaic form of showing off how nice you are is also why today we see names engraved upon park benches, on memorial bricks, and on walls-of-fame at arenas around the world. People want to be known and seen for their altruistic deeds.

If we become a person who helps others, we will be seen. Even if we are a humble person who avoids names on bricks and benches, we will be seen. Become a person who helps others, and your Stone Age antecedent will manifest in the present, and the universe will smile on you.

OVERCOMING OBSTACLES
AND LETTING GO

OUR SOUL IS MORE IMPORTANT THAN OUR IMAGE.

They say bitterness is like drinking poison and hoping the other person will die. Many medical professionals believe that anger, unresolved, is one ingredient that may cause cancer. We don't have to like someone to hang out with them, but when we hold a grudge against someone we do or do not know, we end up accumulating toxic goo in our souls, which only builds up further resentment.

MOVIN' ON ACTION

What does "image isn't as important as your soul" mean to you? Write down your thoughts below.

_____

_____

_____

_____

_____

MOVIN' ON ACTION

If your trying to overcome an obstacle, in your next moving meditation, repeat this simple yet powerful affirmation: "I know I'm going to grow beyond my wildest dreams from this experience."

Again, our lives are based on a series of beliefs. If you have ever watched the Olympics, you've seen mastery in action. Those elite athletes are the result of a series of beliefs acquired throughout their lives. The Olympic athlete's attitude is simple: They show up believing that they will succeed. They show up to life that way. The good news is that you do not need to be an elite athlete to think in this way. You can approach any situation or event with an "I will succeed" mantra.

There is no doubt that Tiger Woods is a gifted golfer, but without his belief in winning, he never would have stayed miles ahead of the competition for so long. What's more interesting was when Woods was faced with a personal growth opportunity. His mindset took a turn, and he began to falter, eventually injuring his back and falling out of the elite ranks.

Today he is back on top and, due to his self-forgiving mindset, and apologizing to those he hurt, it appears (no one knows the heart of another) he has been able to find happiness and community support.

Whether it's due to something you caused (as in Woods's case) or something out of your control, the mind affects the body in the same way. Again, you need not be an elite athlete to experience the highs and lows of achievement, and you can believe your way to living either an illusion or an authentic life.

So, how do we use the athlete's mindset on powerful challenges we will inevitably encounter? How can we use them to get through cancer, the loss of a child, or a bad breakup? Can you become an Ironman triathlete in your world, and train your mind to use self-awareness to capture self-deprecating thoughts and actual physical behaviors, and then switch them out for positivity? I've seen many people achieve this level of self-awareness. There is no doubt in my mind that you can do this.

I have an acquaintance who constantly blames others. In his mind, ev-

---
MOVIN' ON ACTION

Try this the next time you find yourself lonely or lost: simply get up and go where there are people. It could be a church, a gym, a group hike in the woods, a movie, or a good music venue. Just be there and see how you feel. You don't even need to engage in conversation, you just need to be there. If you feel better as a result, then you may understand that the solution to not being lonely or lost is simple: be around healthy people.

---

eryone "screws him over." If he loses his job, the boss screwed him over … if he didn't do well in a race, the equipment was substandard … if a girl doesn't like him, there's something wrong with her. He lacks the ability to be self-aware or introspective and is miserable and lonely. Author Brendan Behan says, "At the innermost core of all loneliness is a deep and powerful yearning for union with one's lost self." The universe will keep firing him from jobs, busting up his relationships, causing him to use the wrong sports equipment, and so on, until he recognizes that it is he himself who is the problem. We don't need to hit rock bottom to grow. In my own experience, however, I have come to learn that getting beat up by the universe allows one the opportunity to increase self-awareness. Has the time come for you to recognize that your life's events and resulting loneliness are manifestations of your inability to find your lost self?

This may seem elementary or even downright silly. The truth is, however, most solutions to movin' on are simple—but the act of doing them may be difficult and even scary.

When one or two people say something negative about you as a person, or about your character, how do you respond? My hope is that you can be somewhat self-aware, and probably, you should just blow it off. However, when you get several people complaining about you (and I'm not referring to a social media pile-on here), maybe it's time to take a deeper look in the mirror. To garner this particular skill requires an abil-

Only a mediocre person is always at their best."
—W. Somerset Maugham

ity to acknowledge what the Bible says: "God is opposed to the proud but gives grace to the humble" (James 4:6). The very act of admitting you were wrong is the fastest way to becoming a happier person. Again, very simple!

How hard is it to crack open that safe in which you have kept your humble self hidden out of fear that you would look weak or vulnerable? There's something super-powerful about admitting to a loved one or work colleague that you've been wrong and asking for forgiveness. This simple act will do more for your relationships than almost anything else.

Imagine a relationship where after a disagreement, you and your spouse (or work colleague) playfully argue about who apologized the fastest and in the sincerest way. How cool would that be?

My good friend, Bunter Knowles, truly leads his life with purpose. He chooses whom he hangs out with, how his house is designed, and what his career path is. He is the most authentic person I know. He owns several acres of land in the city. Over the years, he has received many offers to purchase his land but declined them. It's precious land, but he did not want to give up snowshoeing in his back yard or taking a sauna in the buff for the money. It wasn't worth it! How can you not love that?

PLANT A SHADE TREE, EVEN IF YOU'RE TOO OLD TO EVER ENJOY HER SHADE.

Many years ago, when my son, Beau, was born, I casually asked Bunter if he'd plant a Beau tree with me. He went way out of his way and picked out the best tree, put a fence around it, and even hung a sign that read "Beau's Tree." Now the tree is huge, and I am reminded of what a cool dude he is. My son smiles every time we talk about it. It meant a lot to Beau and me. While I may not see Bunter that much these days, that tree has become a huge symbol of our friendship. He didn't take the attitude of, "If you do something for me, I'll do something for you." He just did it. That's the kind of guy he is.

Maybe you can think of someone you can do this exact same thing for? Who's having a child? Getting married? Graduating? Plant a tree, hang a sign, take a picture. There's no way they won't smile at the very idea of you planting a shade tree, the shade of which you, or the person for whom you are planting the tree, may never even live to enjoy. But, oh, how you'll live on in their memory!

We all know someone like Bunter. I'm talking about the roommate who takes the time to clean up, or the boyfriend who makes you a nice meal when you've had a long day at work. It's the dad who stays up late with the sick kids for the third day in a row, so mom can sleep before going to work the next day. Whenever you can, be that person. Go plant a couple of shade trees! And, while you're at it, name the first one after someone you care about.

SUFFERING LEADS TO REAL-LIFE LESSONS.

I believe that we never forget the emotional experiences in our lives. Further, I believe that some of these experiences change us forever. As for the tough experiences, we do heal, and we can keep movin' on. Heck, I don't want to forget my bad experiences—I'm just happy I'm not the same person I was.

The poet Kahlil Gibran said, "Your pain is the breaking of the shell that encloses your understanding." Real-life suffering leads to real-life lessons. Don't be afraid to use that suffering to reshape your mind.

How can we know when our life is lining up with what the world (or the universe) wants? The first thing to realize is that while we are of the universe, only a portion of us exists in its center. When we're looking at life from a "me" perspective, it's easy to get out of balance and even get addicted to a place where we have felt successful. When others recognized our successes, it fed our ego delicious amounts of confidence. This is one reason why retirement is so hard on people—their unhealthy egos identified themselves with their jobs, and they don't know who they are without them.

Do you ever wonder why great athletes try to make comebacks? For example, why do you think Brett Favre, Michael Jordan, and Lance Armstrong attempted comebacks after they retired? Why did Steve Jobs and others like him come back? For the money? There are many answers, and as author Miguel de Cervantes Saavedra says, "No one knows the heart of another"—but as a fellow athlete, I believe that being in the spotlight and competing on the world stage is what moved them. They felt fulfilled and happiest when they were doing what they were supposed to do. It wasn't for the money.

YOUR EGO FEEDS THE DARKNESS.

The sticky wicket with all of us is finding that sweet balance between fulfillment and ego. To shift from living in our own spotlight (like being an all-knowing parent) to a lonely backstage role (when the kids move out) may require us to humble our heart and take a huge dose of letting go. Perhaps without being in the spotlight, these top athletes and executives felt like they were useless. Given that they had all the money they needed, it wasn't a lack of money that made them come back, but a lack of purpose, the need to be back in the spotlight.

I can relate. It must feel good to get the cheers of huge crowds week after week. But when an inflated ego begins to starve, and the need to feed it gets large and dark, bad decisions and unhealthy behaviors may arise. When you try to recapture faded glory, it can be as grotesque as bringing your dead cat back into the house to play with. Don't get desperate for a past that's not there anymore.

Whether it is retirement, the kids leaving for college, your physical body no longer being able to do what it once could, letting go is a job for the spirit. Again, the mind can navigate the brain through this, if it is totally aware of where it is and what the possibilities are.

Several years ago, I went on a bike ride with my now deceased training buddy, Matt. He had been diagnosed with terminal brain cancer and was told he had two years to live.

Matt was a doctor and incredibly healthy. He had recently finished the Ironman in Wisconsin, had broken three hours in many marathons, completed various Nordic ski marathons, and always ate foods rich in nutrition. In short, he took great care of his health, had three wonderful kids, a wife who was an awesome art teacher (I have one of her pieces in my living room), and friends who loved him. Then, he found out he had cancer.

Normally we joked around a lot. But this ride was different. Those of

---

MOVIN' ON ACTION

Write down some things you need to let go of.

_____

_____

_____

_____

_____

_____

_____

_____

_____

---

you who seriously bike (or run, or ski) understand me when I say you get closer to your endurance sports friends while exercising with them than almost anyone else. Countless hours of saddle time meant we knew each other's life stories, told plenty of dirty jokes, and quarreled over the dumbest things. We had shared the pain of hills and the labored contemplation of our own breathing. Now we shared the truth that one of us was about to die.

As we were spinning along, we hopped from topic to topic. Matt said, "You know what's funny? We used to joke about Christians, but in the past six months this experience has brought me to a real spiritual space." He went on to say that he believes wholeheartedly in the spirit of Jesus. He was charging ahead of me at 26 miles per hour, his scalp, bald from chemotherapy, glowing through his helmet. I asked him to explain (and hoped he'd slow down).

He eased back on the pace and said, "Hmmm … here's what I mean.

Prior to having the golf-ball-sized tumor cut out of my skull, I told the neurosurgeon that if he did a great job cutting the tumor out, I would make him look good. I would be his best patient; I would show up on time, do everything he asked, and follow all the rules … he would never have a more diligent patient."

He went on, "I told the nurses, if you all do your best, I will make you all look really good. I will be the best patient you've ever had. I will eat perfectly, rest when you say rest, do my exercises to spec, and follow all the rules."

I interrupted him, "What does that have to do with Jesus, man?"

He said, "Simple. I was putting the power in the hands of the doctor and his team. The real team is God! True, I had to find a good doc, but all of that is in the hands of the spirit, man."

Can you tell why we got along? Matt was speaking my language.

"I don't believe this doc has any real say in this," he continued. "Yes, he could buy me a few more months, or even years, but the real energy is in living in this moment—right now!"

Matt had never been a religious person, and, while I believed in the spiritual, I was not a follower of any specific doctrine either. But this moment was different … this moment was sacred beyond measure. We biked in silence for the next ten miles. Then we stopped to pee at the side of the road.

As I was peeing, I said, "Look at the gentle person you have become, man. You used to have an edge to you."

"Yeah, I used to be a bit of an angry person," he answered. "I realize now that I was never angry. Look at me now … I am not angry. I just had angry thoughts."

I wondered for a second why it always seemed to take these types of experiences to bring us to a higher state of awareness. Then I realized—that is the mystical. We don't know the "why" until we are in the experience. Facing death, Matt could let go of anger, and after that he was able to shed love all over the place.

But we don't need to know when our time to die is to be present in this moment.

The truth is, we do not know when our time will come. Focus on right now and whenever death comes, it won't be too soon.

MOVIN' ON ACTION

Really stop and think about it. Imagine you found out, beyond any shadow of a doubt, that you would die in six months. Would you keep your same old routine of driving to work, driving home, watching TV, and rinse and repeat? Would you treat your loved ones differently? Would you reconnect with old friends? What would you do?

BUCKET LIST.

After our ride, Matt and I were sitting around the house having a beer, when I asked him the cliché statement, "What's on your bucket list?" He turned to me and said, "Bucket list? You're kiddin' me! I hate that shit! I am not going to fly away on some air balloon or jump off a cliff with a parachute. I don't have a bucket list. I have a fuck-it list!" This meant that he wasn't going to waste a second on things that weren't important.

He said, "I have a four-inch scar above my ear, I have a tumor that may come back. My kids are still fighting, and the sink is clogged with hair ... that's on the list. Even though I can fix it, I called the plumber to take care of it—fuck it! There are judgmental and mean people who used to bug me ... they're on the list. I don't have time for this nonsense—fuck it! I can't bike or run as fast I used to ... on the list. I can still ride—fuck it! The weather has been bad while traveling ... on the list. I can't control that—fuck it!" He went on and on, and we laughed.

As Matt biked away from my house, I watched him, and my eyes started to well up. My mind said, *This may be the last time you see him, man. Remember this moment, take a mental picture.* Then I realized I'd put that on my own "fuck-it list," and made it a point to enjoy the time we had left.

I never saw Matt again, and we didn't finish all our plans together. I got angry with myself. But as Matt would have said, put it on the list...

This world is not my home, I'm just passing through. Matt, I'll see you in that funky space on the other side, or wherever. We're all movin' on!

21

GET HEALTH!

Except for being kept alive a bit too long thanks to modern-day medicine, my grandma lived a very healthy life. She was filled with the kind of spirit and wisdom only a grandma could have. When she was in her late eighties, she experienced a pain in her abdomen. The doctors, without doing any testing, deduced that it was probably cancer and that she had but days to live. Within a few hours, her house was filled with loving and caring people. Most of my cousins, aunts, and uncles, as well as her friends, were there to be with her during her last moments on this earth.

It was an interesting scene. My grandma was asleep in the living room. Everyone else, in true Minnesota style, was in the kitchen telling stories and catching up. As I sat back and observed, I perceived an interesting sense of laughter and overall joyful energy during this time of loss. I was trying to make sense of it. Shouldn't this be a moment filled with sadness and tears? Awkward as it was, this was my family, and I decided to partake in the joy.

Later that afternoon, my grandma mysteriously woke up. We were all perplexed. I went over and asked her how she was doing. She winked at me and said, "The doctors think I am going to die. Ha ha. Let me tell you a secret—I just have gas!"

She lived another half a decade. Like journalist and author Norman Cousins says, "I have learned never to underestimate the capacity of the human mind and body to regenerate—even when prospects seem most wretched. The life force may be the least understood force on earth." Call me wacky, but I truly believe all the laughter and good energy in the room gave her the strength to regenerate. Despite what the doctor said, she had more stories and wisdom to share. Let this be you! Believe in your purpose and ignite your passions, and they will always serve you better.

MOVIN' ON ACTION

GET IN TOUCH WITH YOUR SENSES AND SMILE.

Here's how: Do this Heart-Mind-Muscle (HMM) work-out. If you can, leave your house sometime today and go for a thirty-minute walk or run (heart).

While you are walking, get in touch with your senses and smile (even if you must force it). Stay with the sights, sounds, smells, and smile (mindfulness). After about five minutes, you will begin to feel the increased vibrations that you are bringing into your body. How does it feel? If you focus on what feels good instead of what hurts, you will trigger your mind in a positive way.

When you are done with your walk, do two sets of fifteen push-ups (if you can't do that many in a row, do what you can, as you can, until you get to fifteen). Then do two sets of planks (put your body in the push-up position, but drop down so you're holding yourself up by your elbows, and hold yourself there for thirty seconds), and two sets of fifteen upper back-raises (lying on your stomach with your hands out in airplane position, lift your thumbs to the sky as high as you can, squeezing the shoulder blades together) (muscle).

When you are done, perform the following stretches to the point of mild discomfort:

1. Inverted hurdler stretch. Sit down and pull your left foot toward your groin. Keeping your back flat, gently bring your belly toward your right thigh. Hold for twenty seconds. Switch feet.
2. Butterfly stretch. Sitting down, bring the base of both feet together at your groin. Keeping your back flat, lean forward while simultaneously pressing down with your el-

MOVIN' ON ACTION

bows on both knees. Hold for twenty seconds.

3. Lying-down quad stretch. Lying on your right side, grab your left ankle and gently bring your left foot toward your rear end. Hold for twenty seconds. Switch feet.

4. Low back stretch. Lying on your back, pull your right knee toward your chest. Hold for twenty seconds. Switch sides.

5. Cobra stretch. Lying on your belly, put your hands in the push-up position just outside your chest. Keeping your hip bones on the floor, gently push upward, stretching the muscles of the stomach.

While you are doing your exercises, it's very important that you mindfully think of what beliefs you have toward exercise. Write these beliefs down. Maybe you think exercise is a waste of time, or that it's for kids. Maybe you think you can't possibly exercise because you haven't done it in 40 years! Maybe you believe exercise is painful or can only happen in the gym, or perhaps, hopefully, you see exercise as fun and energizing. Whatever your beliefs are, if they support you moving your body for at least forty-five minutes a day, then they are beliefs you can embrace.

If exercise is new for you, then you need to keep your mind on high alert to recognize when a negative belief that keeps you from moving enters your mind. By being aware of such negative beliefs, you will flex your by-now-stronger meditation muscles, and gently cast those beliefs out.   You'll rule out any need for an iron will—and be able to do it gently, if you approach it the right way!

Intellectual knowledge is conducive to change only inasmuch as it is also effective knowledge."
—*Baruch Spinoza*

ASSOCIATE PLEASURE WITH EXERCISE.

Let's make this practical. Are you living a life filled with energy? If you love to bike, walk, kayak, stand-up paddleboard, or just poke around new places, you will find yourself moving forward. If you are not feeling a good connection with your physical body, it is time to commit passion toward changing that.

Find a qualified trainer and hire him or her for three to four weeks. This will get you through the discipline phase, and you will learn the right techniques and intensity to have a safe experience. A trainer might seem expensive, but remember that you either pay now in cash or later in hospital visits and blood-pressure medication. You will be surprised at how valuable this investment in exercise knowledge will be.

Creating a new habit of exercising regularly is an act of the unconscious. Your unconscious needs to associate pleasure with movement, or else it will merely remain an intellectual act and not an effective experience.

It's your body—love it! If you exercise, eat well, and, most importantly, get enough sleep, you will enjoy the true treasures of life much better.

IF YOU REALLY NEED TO MAKE A CHANGE, GET OUT OF YOUR TOWN.

Seeing something different, even if only for two weeks, is a sure way to get out of a rut or to recharge your batteries. When you travel, you look at different things, smell different smells, taste different foods, hear different sounds, and feel different energies. Travel recharges the brain, and it is healthy. You don't need to go to the Bahamas or other faraway places to enjoy the things that shake up your senses. You just need to get up and go somewhere different.

I was in Costa Rica recently where I met an old man wearing an orange cloth around his head, baggy clothes, and was surrounded in an aura of mystery. As I engaged him in simple conversation, I came to realize he was a modern-day guru and was projecting a sense of calm that made me want to talk all day. While we talked about everything from spiritual issues to the New England Patriots football team, the thing he told me that resonated the most was what he does, when he does it, and why.

His name was Majji. He taught a form of yoga called Kundalini, and he was clearly not a poser. He was over 70 years old and super-fit. His skin practically glowed, and a smile was permanently glued to his face. While I knew a little about what Kundalini yoga was, I asked him to explain it to me.

He talked about how the Kundalini energy is like a snake that comes up from the belly. He talked about the importance of doing the practice before the earth awakens. It turns out he taught the class every morning at 4:45 am to a group of followers. By practicing Kundalini yoga before the earth awakens, he said, you can enter an energy portal that gets busy and blocked once the sun—and the rest of the sentient beings—wakes up.

In short, when traveling, I met an interesting man! He shared an insight that was meaningful to me. I now practice my own form of meditation, before the sun rises, several times per week.

PLAY.

Many of my most memorable moments, my greatest experiences, and most of my business ideas have come to me in the course of play, long workouts, or unplanned travels. The restaurant ideas, events, fitness-training secrets, seminar insights, and my observation of the traits of happy people have come about simply by Movin' around this planet.

It is strange that many people struggle to take more than a week or two off for a trip per year. Worse, when they travel, they go somewhere "safe" and predictable. If this is you, I encourage you to step outside of your norm, "stretch" your courage, and go somewhere that has the potential to expand your mind. Meet people of different cultures. Stop and really look at the landscape around you. Eat something wacky and weird. You may find yourself truly loving these experiences and creating a new self that is at home with diverse cultures, full of interesting stories, and inspired by new ideals. And most importantly, you're rewiring your brain into new and different pathways.

MOVIN' ON ACTION

Write down and go (in the next week) to one place you have never been that would stimulate your senses. It doesn't have to be a faraway place. It could be the local aquarium, museum or park. While you are at it try getting up before dawn and see how your five senses are affected by the awakening of the day. Write down how it feels.

_____

_____

_____

_____

_____

_____

If you have a huge gash in your leg, chances are you won't ignore it, even for a minute. If you say you're too busy to deal with it and try to let it go, you will find yourself in the hospital with a serious infection. Instead, you'll take the necessary steps to prevent your body from getting infected.

Do we put the same intensity on emotional or psychological cuts or gashes? Research shows that people with severe depression in developing countries associate that depression with pains in the body. For example, a person in West Africa suffering from depression may say, "I feel sick in my stomach," rather than, "I feel really sad." In developed countries, we say the pain is in our head and/or emotions. But the metaphors can be similar; in developed countries we may say that someone has a "broken heart," or that something "made me sick to my stomach." Sometimes our emotions can cause physical pain without us realizing it.

MOVIN' ON ACTION

Let's find out if you are you holding stress.

Sit comfortably in your chair. Take a very deep breath, shrug and hold your shoulders tensing your trapezius muscles toward your ears. After four seconds, release the breath, and, with your mind, relax all the muscles you tensed. Repeat three times. Now rank the feeling on a scale of 1 to 5.

☐ 1   ☐ 2   ☐ 3   ☐ 4   ☐ 5

One means you didn't feel any form of relaxation and five means you felt as though your head was floating off your neck. If you said a 3 or higher, you are holding tension.

Keep in mind you simply used your mind to tell your cardiovascular system to bring blood filled with oxygen to those tight muscles, which means the opposite is happening when you are not aware.

Let me be clear: The pain in your lower back could be the result of workplace stress. The crick in your neck may come from your divorce. Do not blow this statement off! Your chronic headaches might just disappear if only you can rid yourself of the toxic relationships, environments, and debilitating beliefs that may be causing them. Sometimes the heart can cure what the pain pills cannot.

IS THE PAIN IN YOUR BODY A DISTRACTION?

In 1981, Dr. John Sarno published a paper in the Journal of Nervous and Mental Disease regarding back and neck pain. Dr. Sarno discovered "that most back and neck pain is due to a psycho physiological process in muscle and nerve tissue known as tension myositis syndrome (TMS)." Basically, he found that stress and/or suppressed emotions were a psychosomatic pain that manifested in the neck and/or back.

Yes, the pain is real. Yes, if you do an X-ray or MRI you may see compressed nerves, bulged discs, etc. What is interesting is that the research shows there are equally as many people who do not have back or neck pain, yet have all the same structural problems, such as scoliosis and bulging discs, as those in pain. So why aren't those folks limping around in pain?

According to this theory, the brain believes that a pain in the back is preferable to dealing with the pain of guilt for missing your grandma's funeral to play golf with your friends. Specifically, the brain tells the nerves to pinch off blood flow to the neck and back, creating a painful muscle tension as a means to distract your attention from emotions that seem too tough to deal with. Some researchers call this "distraction pain syndrome (DPS)," instead of TMS.

In short, our chronic daily problems are causing our pain. The longer you stay in this pattern, the more you engage the nervous system. Once the nervous system receives these messages, oxygen deprivation and muscle tension begins.

I had a lower-back problem several years ago after I was faced with a personal crisis that led me to a high level of situational depression. I had two back surgeries in my lumbar area to free up a nerve that was being compressed. The second surgery was successful. A year later, however, I started feeling the same symptoms again. I went to the same neurosurgeon, who had been studying TMS, and after looking at the MRIs he concluded that there was no pressed nerve. What is remarkable is that after he told me that, a good half of my pain went away instantly.

I was so relieved, yet frustrated. As an athlete who competed on the international stage, I was upset with myself. I thought, *How in the heck did I allow my brain to bring this pain to my body?* I know now what led to my back pain. I was an emotional wreck. Those emotions led to strong physical pain.

Maybe you're in a similar situation. Without a great therapist to rally you through these emotions and invite you to deal with them head-on, your mind will train your brain to create pain to distance you from dealing with the emotional problems. Don't let this happen to you. Get real with your emotions. If you are a tough personality who says, "This is hogwash," then you will not improve. If you are a passive person who simply sticks your head in the sand, then you will get a sandy result. With that said, be aware that whenever you are dealing with high-level stress, you need to understand that if you don't deal with it head-on, the results will not be pretty. It's like the person who doesn't want to quit smoking but

---

MOVIN' ON ACTION

Three steps to overcoming Distraction Pain Syndrome (DPS) in the neck and lower back:

1. Start thinking like a psychologist. Deliberately communicate to your own mind that you can beat the sub- conscious and its little distraction strategy. For example, if you have lower-back pain, on your next walk, think to yourself, "I'm happy and I'm pain-free." Start visualizing the blood flowing through your back, lubricating it, and creating effortless movement.
2. Think fresh, clean thoughts. Learn to use behaviors and thoughts to stop suppressing emotion. For example, say to yourself, "I'm going to mindfully let go of the stresses at work and not allow that to create my back pain." Feel your body release its grip on you.
3. Incorporate an alternative therapy, like journaling, yoga, or hiring a mind-body therapist.

When you move from a casual, temporary approach toward a thoughtful, focused approach, your lower-back pain will be reduced, or better yet, gone!
When you start to become stressed, first become aware of your general tension patterns.

---

joins a smoking-cessation program. It's not going to happen. Following these steps will work if you believe in them. I wanted to get better, so I did some research on this subject, and it totally convinced me. If you need some more persuasion, I encourage you to consider this for yourself.

HOW TO DE-STRESS—NOW!

Years ago, a colleague, Dr. Robert Cooper, taught me his Instant Calming Sequence (ICS). He said that when you are faced with a stressful situation, your body goes through many physiological processes to protect you. You hold your breath, tighten your muscles, crunch forward in your posture, and scowl. In the ICS, he has you reverse these debilitating responses. Once you learn this technique, you can de-stress in an instant.

MOVIN' ON ACTION

De-stress now. Here's how it works:

If someone cuts you off on the highway (to use an example), the first thing you need to do is to maintain deep breathing. Simply imagine your breath reaching all the way down to the bottom of your lungs. Second, imagine a wave of relaxation running through your whole body, top to bottom. Like the scanner at the grocery store, imagine a red beam of light passing from head to toe, relaxing every muscle along the way. Third, sit up or stand in a good posture. Bring your shoulders back, suck your gut in a bit, and place equal weight on each foot (or both sitting bones). Fourth, smile. Allow the corners of your mouth to curl up, and the crow's feet at the corners of your eyes to wrinkle up.

If you are smiling at the poor driver pulling out in front of you while sitting up straight, relaxing the gripping muscles in the chest and back, and breathing deeply, you will have the space to acknowledge the fifth step—the reality of the situation. Maybe the person is not a jerk. Maybe he is in a hurry because his wife is having a baby, or because he is late for work. Who knows? And moreover, it doesn't matter!

Dr. Robert Cooper's Instant Calming Sequence (ICS):

1. Breathe.
2. Wave of relaxation.
3. Maintain good posture.
4. Smile.
5. Acknowledge reality.

SEIZE THE DAY!

My mentor and great friend, Richard Haney, once threw a party for his now-deceased wife, Pat. Prior to her death, the doctors told her that she had days, if she was lucky maybe months, to live. Rather than stay at home huddled in misery and wallowing in their well-deserved sadness, they decided to invite a few friends over and celebrate her birthday.

When I arrived at the party, I was taken aback. The cars were lined up and down the street as far as the eye could see. There were people there that I hadn't seen for many years. How had Richard been able to get hold of all these people? Some of the people having fun together hadn't spoken to each other in years. I couldn't believe it. The energy this celebration of Pat's life had created allowed old friends to heal their broken relationships and new friendships to form. There were family members embracing. There was an old-fashioned spirit of laughter and positive energy throughout the crowd. It was happiness at the highest level. Love was in the air!

How wonderful that Pat was there to witness it!

CAN YOU CHANGE YOUR MIND?

My elder son, Beau, has type 1 diabetes. He and I were traveling to Costa Rica when he was in his early teens, and after a long trip of flight transfers, long airport layovers, dehydration, and heat, we finally arrived at our hotel. We were both absolutely beat. We showered, ate some supper, and crashed. Beau is very good about managing his diabetes, and neither his mom nor I need to worry about him. However, round about midnight I woke up to some loud huffing sounds. I looked over at my son in the bed next to me and noticed he was in a diabetic coma. I couldn't

No one has ever loved anyone the way everyone wants to be loved."

—*Mignon McLaughlin*

wake him up, and I had no idea what to do.

I looked for his Glucagon pen and quickly realized he forgot to pack it. I looked for sugar, but there was no way he could take it in his passed-out state. My whole being was searching for solutions. I went to the office and screamed for help. Jonathan, my Costa Rican friend who owned the place, woke up and came to the rescue. Without hesitation, he quickly grabbed my young boy, flipped him over his shoulder like a big bag of rice, and began running to the clinic. Once there, they administered glucose, and within a few minutes, my son woke up.

The next day, Beau was ready to surf, feed the monkeys, and experience all the wonders Costa Rica had to offer. While he learned a valuable lesson from the experience, he didn't dwell on it. He had let go and moved on. I, on the other hand, was still freaking out! Sometimes you must think like a child and let it go.

Years ago, before 9/11, my roommate, Thomas, and I were competing in the Lanzarote Ironman triathlon in the Canary Islands. While we were racing, our hotel room was totally ransacked. The bandits took my passport and all our credit cards and money. We had planned to fly out the next day and didn't know what to do. Thomas was flying to Europe, and I was going back to the U.S. Fortunately, they didn't get Thomas's passport, and $10 was hidden in his pants. I reported the theft to the police, but the only thing they could do was give me a copy of their report in hopes that it might serve as my passport to get me off the island and to the American Embassy in Madrid. It was clear sailing for Thomas, since he still had a passport, and airplanes served food back then. He gave me the $10 and a pat on the back. "Good luck, man!"

**Carpe diem, quam minimum credula postero.
Seize the day, and place minimal trust in the
morrow."**

—*Horace*

YOU CAN ALWAYS SEE THE GOOD.

I was able to use my Minnesota smile and the police report to board the plane from Lanzarote to Madrid. However, they would not let me fly from Madrid to the U.S. without a passport. I needed to get to the Embassy in Madrid.

Once I arrived in Madrid, I was told that the Embassy would close at 5:00 pm and that it wouldn't be open the next day. I landed at 3:00 pm, and it is a two-hour bus ride to the Embassy. I didn't have enough money for a taxi, so I had no option. I got off the plane and booked it to the bus station. I quickly caught the bus, and along the way sent out huge intentions to speed our progress.

It seemed as though the bus driver was stopping at every intersection to say, "Hola!" to some friend or relative. "Hurry up, man!" I thought. As I sat there wearing this "What am I going to do tonight if I don't get to the Embassy?" sort of smile on my face, I knew at that moment that today would be a day I'd never forget. The guy sitting next to me must have read my smile. He said, in English, "What are you up to? You seem like you have a lot on your mind."

I told him my story, and he said he would help. His name was Matt, and he had just arrived from Seattle aiming to learn Spanish.

"That is super-cool, man!" I told him. He talked to the bus driver, and before you know it we were cruising at warp speed. The driver dropped us off right at the U.S. Embassy at 4:55 p.m. We ran like crazy, and just like the movies, we dove in as the door was closing. "I made it!"

The guy at the Embassy was very cool and helpful. He contacted Visa and got me a copy of my passport. I would be able to get cash the next day, as well as catch my flight. Though I only had a few dollars to my name, I took a huge breath of relief, and my new friend Matt and I high-fived.

What happened next is truly amazing. Matt didn't have a place lined up that night, other than to call a friend of a friend. He called, and she said her place was super-small, but we could both stay there. Great! I had a free place to stay, and all was good. The three of us went out and grabbed a bite to eat. It was a warm, eighty-degree night, and we decided to walk the streets of Madrid. Matt loaned me some money. We sat down on a park bench, and I shared the events of the past twenty-four hours. We laughed.

Just then, we heard the most amazing guitar sounds. We looked over, and Matt's friend was screaming with joy. She told us that the world's greatest flamenco guitar player was doing an impromptu concert right there in front of us. For the first three minutes, we were the only ones there. Within twenty minutes, there were thousands of onlookers and admirers. I couldn't believe it. What a treat!

I had to thank the bandits for giving me this opportunity to move on from the fear of not getting home and to have the time of my life. Through this world-class experience, I made new friendships and garnered memories I'll still be sharing when I'm 80!

REMEMBER, YOU CAN CHOOSE HOW TO RESPOND TO EVERYTHING THAT HAPPENS TO YOU.

Not everyone who lives their authentic life experiences automatic joy. I have a friend who is gay and sometimes felt the world was against him. I asked him what I could do to help—to make him feel like society is on the mend, increasingly able to be kinder toward him and the rest of the gay community. He told me to go out to the world and "Live out loud." In other words, don't laugh at the sarcastic or demeaning jokes. Be the one in the crowd who speaks up against the tyranny of innuendos and subtleties. Speak up against those who harbor hatred toward the gay (or any other) community.

YOU TEACH PEOPLE HOW TO TREAT YOU.

Remember, we teach people how to treat us. I can guarantee that if you use the above MOA even once, that person will think twice before telling a racist joke around you again. Their conscious mind may think of you as a prude or someone too serious to take a joke, but their subconscious mind will anchor you as a person of conviction, integrity, and virtue.

MOVIN' ON ACTION

If someone tells a joke in poor taste, simply say, "I don't understand what you mean by (insert racist line here)."

When we're trying to understand the perspectives of others, we need to find a balance between flexible and solid. It's like a tree: if we are too rigid, like an oak, the high winds will blow us over; but if we are too flexible, like a palm, a small truck backing into us will break us in two. If we choose to laugh along with the crowd at a racist joke, we're being too flexible. If we jump down someone's throat and assign them a smug label like "bigot" without seeking to first show some compassion or talk them out of it, we're being too rigid.

Live for seeding your virtues in other people's subconscious minds. You'll never go wrong in the long run!

EMBRACING OUR TRUE PURPOSE.

Rod Raymond with son, Jack Moran: I've shared my friends' stories, their challenges, and achievements, but I'd like to close this book with a story that affected me on a transpersonal level.

Getting to the Ironman World Championships in Hawaii is a lifelong dream for most triathletes. I had been there three times before. Seeing old friends, and making new ones, is always the best. However, there was something particularly special about my fourth Ironman in 2000, which helped me embrace my true purpose. This day was one of the most meaningful days in my life, and it changed my awareness forever.

The timing of this triathlon wasn't quite as I'd wished it to be. The demands of work and family prior to the race were at an all-time high. My training hours were cut in half, and I had a pulled hamstring. However, what made it "perfect" was that my old girlfriend, Sarah, told me we were expecting a surprise baby...

I was spinning. I had an amazing opportunity that I was about to embark upon, and at the same time, I had learned that I was about to become a dad again. I was so distracted that I thought that maybe I should just drop out of the race. Instead, I took Steve Prefontaine's advice: "To give anything less than your best is to sacrifice the gift."

BLEND AND HARMONIZE WITH ALL
THAT COMES TO YOU.

As all athletes know, there is a nervousness that blends with excitement before a race. While the world's best athletes stretched, jogged, and checked and re-checked their gear all around me, I chose to lie down next to my bike, close my eyes and reflect on what was to become of this day. While I had plenty of experience in visualization, at that time I had very little training in meditation. I was purposefully attempting to release my attachments and expectations surrounding the race.

Lying on the ground peacefully, I remembered my aikido instructor, Dr. Frank Guldbrandson, telling me to let my energy flow through me. He said, "Find the mental and physical tools necessary to locate your center, and then blend and harmonize with all that comes to you. First see it, feel it—then harmonize or flow with it."

As I got up off the ground, I was centered and focused. Come what may, I was ready. There was such a calm, such detachment.

I said to myself, "Just breathe and smile … just breathe and smile." At that moment, I realized there would be no magic, no secret pill, no one to give me a motivational speech. I simply needed to open myself up and allow the race to happen.

I put on my swim cap and goggles and then stepped into the water to warm up. Down near the ocean floor, a stingray the size of a small car gently glided by. I waved to get the other athletes to look down, but they were so focused they didn't seem to notice.

Alone with the stingray, I finally saw the way forward. My race, my life, my future at that moment was all about gliding. If I could swim effortlessly and without desire, I knew I would find flow. For the first time in my life, I felt at one with the ocean.

The gun went off. Athletes were banging into me, but I just "blended and harmonized" with their aggressive energy.

I felt amazing—I really was gliding! As I passed through the swim finish, I looked at the clock and realized I'd just had one of my fastest swim splits ever. At this point, I knew I was going to have a physically and spiritually transforming day.

As I made my way through the swim-to-bike transition area, among a sea of adults, I noticed an enthusiastic little girl trying her best to pass me some water. Why was she focusing on me—amidst a stream of more than twenty athletes exiting the water at that moment? I couldn't help but think of that Bible verse in Mark, Chapter 10, about "childlike faith." I just needed to have the faith of a child. I took the ice-cold water from the excited little girl and thanked her for the lesson.

When I got on my bike, my arms ached, the taste of sea salt was nauseating, and it was above ninety degrees. With 112 miles of biking and 26.2 miles of running to go, I needed to be cautious in how I managed my energy. I was being passed, left and right, by adrenaline-pumped athletes going too fast, but I let it go.

As the race went on, I began to catch up again. At the forty-mile mark, the bike course ran parallel with the ocean. The trade winds blowing off the ocean were dangerously high, with gusts reaching 50 mph. Professional athletes were getting blown off their bikes all around me, and one even broke his collarbone. My mind was racing faster than I was. *Was I going to crash? Would the sight of athletes crashing around me affect my flow?* With my "blending and harmonizing" mantra, I mindfully leaned my bike at the perfect angle into the wind and pedaled faster.

This was not the time to glide, so I flexed with the wind and maneuvered through its gusts. I felt in peak state and continued to pass the athletes, one after another.

As I finished the bike leg, I looked up at the clock and realized that I just biked one of the top splits of this world-class race. I was truly in flow, and it felt like a dream. What the heck was going on? I didn't think I was in peak form.

The last event was the marathon, a 26.2-mile course in the sweltering heat. Thousands of spectators watch this race, and I saw many of them as I ran through ancient lava fields and small villages. For me, harnessing the energy of the spectators was more powerful than any ergogenic aid out there. It was as though the fans were willing me to do my best.

MASTERY IS DOING SOMETHING EFFORTLESSLY.

Eighteen miles in, my confidence was growing as I ran past some of the world's top athletes. Time stood still, and there was no pain. Often, I tend to push harder and harder. If something is too easy, I feel a little guilty or undeserving. At this moment, however, I had total clarity. My mind, body, and soul were free.

My free mind enabled me to experience both bliss and clarity. How would I bond with my soon-to-be-born son? Would my relationship with his mother be healthier now that we weren't together anymore? I hoped the peak feelings would last.

Four miles later, the crisis came. I was exhausted, covered in sweat, and breathing hard. Other runners started to pass me. My inner voice began screaming, "Don't get passed! Don't bonk now! Go faster! Hold your position!"

The louder my ego got, the worse I felt, and the slower I ran. I needed a change. I had to recall what Lao-tzu said in the *Tao Te Ching*: "The master's power is this: He lets all things come and go effortlessly, without desire; he never expects results; thus, he is never disappointed."

Who cares if I win or lose—who cares if I even finish? I was going to have fun, detach from expectations, and be present. Mystically, I regained my energy and hung on for four miles. As I was nearing the finish area, the spectators' cheers were like a rock concert.

With two hundred yards to go, a voice over the intercom told me I was second in my age group. I slowed down and began high-fiving spectators and friends along the final stretch—pure ego! As I casually jogged across the finish line, a German competitor in my age class came racing by. We crossed the line side-by-side! I had no idea he was coming up on me. Did I just lose my second-place position?

It was my final test of the day. My ego told me to get angry about maybe placing third, but I shoved it aside and said, "No expectations!" It wasn't until later in the day that I chose to look at the results. I'd gotten second place by one-tenth of a second in my age group after all.

The Ironman Triathlon is more than a physical challenge. For anyone who allows the full experience to manifest, the race is transformational. Today I strive to remain present in my daily walk and to embrace the full embodiment of life's experiences. My son Jack is a grown teen now and is happy and content living in Florida with his mom, step dad and sister.

EPILOGUE
MOVIN' ON, MOVIN' FORWARD

There is no coming to consciousness without pain.
—C. G. Jung

Whether it be a relationship, a job, a disease, financial woes, or whatever, everyone, sooner or later, needs some movin' on from something. But maybe a better idea is "movin' forward."

I began the book with this quote:

What if we could blend and harmonize with life's celebrations and inevitable despairs? What if we got past the idea that we could only be happy once every problem was fully solved? Perhaps happiness means accepting the good with the bad, and using the bad to bring forth the good? As Buddhist philosophy states, "Suffer what there is to suffer, rejoice in what there is to rejoice."

You may have heard the adage that the truth is irreversible. If you believe this, then any fake rumors about you are reversible. In recent years, the Catholic Church acknowledged that Galileo wasn't a heretic. It's true that some people will probably never accept truth. For these folks, we can only offer our compassion, and hope that one day their inflexibility will turn around.

For myself and my kids, I hope we continue to understand that owning what is wrong and moving forward making it right leads to joy and guilt-free living. To live with anger, hatred, or any other debilitating emotion will lead you straight down the road of despair. If there's been one underlying message in this book, it's that there is far more value in seeking meaning than in finding meaning. Can you use a trauma to forge a greater meaning in your life? Of course you can! Can you turn your adversities into victories? Of course you can! Now, the question is: Will we do this mindful work, and then do it some more?

It is important for us to find a liberating vocabulary. The voice in our head is real, and while it may keep us up at night, it can also get us going

> **Think to yourself that every day is your last; the hour to which you do not look forward will come as a welcome surprise."**
>
> —*Horace*

in the morning. The energy to change is in the mystical, the spirit, your God. This energy is drawn into our universe, our cells, and it can manifest itself in many ways.

We were put here to make this world a better place. What a great responsibility!

For me, I'm here for a reason (or reasons) I'm not sure I am even aware of. By continuing to be mindful and staying awake to what is happening for me, I feel I can be my best self. I know I am going to continue to have a ball experiencing the ambiguities in my life. What I have truly come to understand in my short life, is that having fun may be served best not only by movin' on, but by movin' toward an inner knowing that understands the difference.

SIX TYPES OF MEDITATION

1. Concentrated, or focused, meditation.

Do this while sitting in a comfortable position. Put both feet on the ground, keep your posture erect, and close your eyes, or just look softly ahead of you. After a few short minutes, begin focusing on your breath. Focus on the air coming into the nose and passing out of the mouth. After a few breaths, begin to count to ten, starting with one. As you count, breathe in for five counts and out for five counts. If a distracting thought comes along while counting, go back to one. It is very important that you do not get agitated or frustrated if your brain wanders off. This is very normal, and the act of going back to your breath is the "workout." You can start with five minutes a day and work up to as long as you want. The key is to stay concentrated or focused on breathing.

2. Mindfulness meditation

As famed professor and founder of the Stress Reduction Clinic Jon Kabat-Zinn says, "Mindfulness means paying attention, in a particular way; on purpose, in the present moment, and non-judgmentally." In this technique, you may stop to enjoy a sunset or listen to children laugh in a more purposeful, soul-filling kind of way. Simply put, mindfulness meditation is just a way of saying "I'm going to be mindful at this moment." You don't even need to call it meditation. I use "being aware" or "being awake" interchangeably with mindfulness throughout this book. The best way to become mindful is to imagine your thoughts are taking an elevator ride from your head to your gut. Once in your gut, you can sense the world in a more meaningful way.

3. Reflective, or open meditation, technique

The reflective, or open method, of meditation is where you reflect on a topic and perhaps come to a realization that you may not have been aware of already. The best way to get into this method is to sit comfortably, bring your attention to your breathing, and clear your mind. After your mind is clear, be open to what comes into your mind regarding that specific topic on which you're seeking wisdom. Reflect on it, and see what insights emerge.

4. Creative, or purposeful, meditation

In creative meditation, you consciously and purposely explore a specific quality of your mind. The best way to get into this method is to sit comfortably, bring your attention to your breathing, and clear your mind. Once the mind is cleared, bring in the quality you wanted to explore. Just be creative with this quality, and see what answers arise. "How can I be more patient?" can be the question going into this meditation.

5. Moving meditation

Because I am an active person, this form of meditation is my favorite. The best way to do it is to go for a walk, jog, or bike ride in nature. As you move, focus on your breath, as with focused meditation. Inhale while counting from one to five, and exhale while counting from six to ten. Feel the wind on your face, the earth under your shoes, and the sounds of the critters around you. As a thought comes along, gently recognize it, and either let it go, or mark it in some way for correction later (i.e., if it's an angry thought or negative voice). By using the energy that is stirred up by your bodily motion, you can connect to breath and nature in an effort to free your mind of toxic thoughts and other energies that do not serve you.

6. Oral meditation

This form of meditation is said aloud. For example, when you chant verbally to anchor a mantra or repeat a statement to retrain the brain, you are using a form of oral meditation.

Regardless of which meditation you use. When you find the one that brings the most awareness for you, that is the right one. And, like I say to my clients when they ask what the best exercise is, "Do the one that you will actually do!"

50 TIPS FOR MOVIN' ON

Over the years, I have talked to hundreds of people who have experienced moments of challenge and learned what steps they took to grow from those challenges. The following fifty statements are a summary of this wisdom. Include them in your daily meditation, add more as you see fit, and we will all keep movin' on!

1. Be your authentic self; you are supposed to be here.
2. Trust your gut feelings but be careful how you decipher them.
3. Avoid saying anything negative in the media (social or mainstream). There's an old proverb that says, "One can pay back the loan of gold, but one lives forever in debt to those who are kind."
4. Volunteer for something you care about.
5. Be confident enough to say, "No."
6. Don't be afraid to say, "Yes."
7. Go easy on yourself—you're all you've got.
8. Get a dog or cat, care for it, and spend time with it.
9. Don't take what others say about you personally, and only say kind things about others. As an unknown author wrote, "Kind words can be short and easy to speak, but their echoes are truly endless."
10. Keep moving forward, deliberately doing what you want to do.
11. Exercise every time you feel anxious or depressed. Yes, this may mean a walk at 3 a.m.!
12. Sleep, but don't lie around moping.
13. Eat well but avoid overeating.
14. Practice yoga or another contemplative practice.

15. Surround yourself with people who care about you and who don't judge your past.

16. If it feels wrong, make your life easier by not doing it.

17. Don't assume everyone knows your situation. They don't.

18. Eat more fruits and vegetables. They are the catalysts for good energy.

19. Never talk badly about yourself—even if you're only talking to yourself.

20. Get out of your comfort zone as much as you can and consciously surround yourself with those who are supportive.

21. Let go of what you cannot control. Say, "This is like the weather, I cannot control it."

22. Reconnect with family members you haven't seen in a while.

23. Stay away from drama and negativity, both face-to-face and on social media. Do not read blogs or engage in debates that speak negatively about you or others. If confronted, say, "I'm sorry you feel that way, I know differently."

24. Connect to nature by simply sitting next to a tree or gazing into a pond or lake. Nature will never judge you and will always listen.

25. Get into therapy and find professional third-party help, if necessary.

26. Say what you mean as directly and precisely as possible, both to yourself and others. Follow your words into purposeful and direct action.

27. Explore your purpose and meaning and live to that end.

28. Understand that you are not that important. People have more important things to do than to talk about you.

29. Understand that the media (social and mainstream) is temporary. Humans have a very short-term memory and are on to the next issue within a few days. In other words, say this mantra, "This too shall pass."

30. Truly believe that your higher self only wants happiness for you—live in partnership with that self.

31. Acknowledge that finding peace of mind or enlightenment does not mean that all your pains are behind you and only bliss awaits you in the future. It means that bliss is in your future, and all future pains are seeds that will grow into something that will serve you.

32. Recognize that you do not have the strength to hold your pain for-

ever and make the decision to set it down. You may have to "set it down" in your mind a hundred times before it becomes a habit.

33. Meditate at least fifteen minutes a day to strengthen your awareness "muscles," so you have the strength to catch any debilitating thoughts or actions that can hinder your growth. Max Planck said, "The energy of consciousness affects the outcomes."

34. If something feels forced, it probably is. Learn to respect this feeling. The healthy mind never forces and always allows.

35. Stay happy in the present, for all you have is this moment right now. "One day at a time" might more appropriately be phrased "One moment at a time."

36. Be aware of negative thoughts about yourself and others and create a new voice that reframes and converts the inner conversation to a positive one.

37. Send compassion to someone you do not like or respect.

38. When difficult emotions emerge, gently recognize them, and breathe, walk, meditate, self-talk, or whatever you must do to help them along on their way out of you.

39. Practice body scanning (head to toe) to remove any tightness in your body that harbors tension and debilitating emotions.

40. Create a garden or volunteer to plant trees. Find an activity in nature that fosters growth.

41. Consciously send compassion in your thoughts, actions, or prayers to others who you know are in pain.

42. Keep a daily journal and go back and read it. If need be, burn it for complete surrender.

43. It's okay to start over if you fall. It's okay to start over if…

44. Use ordinary moments to make you smile—even if you must fake it. Philosopher Alan Watts said, "Zen does not confuse spirituality with thinking about God while one is peeling potatoes. Zen spirituality is just to peel the potatoes." Find happiness in the ordinary.

45. Laugh as much as you can; it's truly the best medicine.

46. Avoid those who suck your energy. It is not theirs, it's yours, and you get to choose how to share it.

47. Travel alone to a place far away from those who know you. Look at new people, new things, and new cultures, meet friends, and develop a

new way of thinking and being. Create the stories that you will tell when you're too old to travel.

48. Understand that emotional pain is like a wound: it will get better, and, if you are lucky, you might even have a scar that can remind you of how you grew from the experience.

49. Never give up on your dreams but reframe them if the reality of accomplishing them no longer exists.

50. Make peace with the fact that your life is but a vapor that will vanish in the wind and choose to live right now. The healing comes from creating a space in this moment for all these things to happen.

Problems come together and then they collapse. After what you have read here, ask yourself: "Are there really any problems?"

KEEP IT EASY ... JUST KEEP MOVIN' ON!

CPSIA information can be obtained
at www.ICGtesting.com
Printed in the USA
BVHW031441091221
623630BV00011B/493

9 780971 882010